BUILDING YOUR OWN
NATURE MUSEUM

By Vinson Brown

The Amateur Naturalist's Diary
The Amateur Naturalist's Handbook
Backyard Wild Birds of California and the Pacific Northwest
The Californian Wildlife Region (*with George Lawrence*)
California Wildlife Map Book (*with David Hoover*)
Exploring Pacific Coast Tide Pools
Handbook of California Birds (*with Henry Weston, Jr.*)
How to Explore the Secret Worlds of Nature
How to Follow the Adventures of Insects
How to Make a Miniature Zoo
Investigating Nature Through Outdoor Projects
Native Americans of the Pacific Coast
The Pomo Indians of California and Their Neighbors
Reading the Woods
Reptiles and Amphibians of the West
Rocks and Minerals of California (*with David Allan and James Stark*)
Sea Mammals and Reptiles of the Pacific Coast
The Sierra Nevadan Wildlife Region (*with Robert Livezey*)
Warriors of the Rainbow (*with William Willoya*)
Wildlife and Plants of the Cascades (*with Charles Yocom*)
Wildlife in the Intermountain West (*with Charles Yocom and Aldine Starbuck*)

BUILDING YOUR OWN
NATURE MUSEUM
For Study and Pleasure

VINSON BROWN

Illustrated by Don Greame Kelley

ARCO PUBLISHING, INC.
NEW YORK

Published by Arco Publishing, Inc.
215 Park Avenue South, New York, N.Y. 10003

Library of Congress Cataloging in Publication Data

Brown, Vinson, 1912–
    Building your own nature museum: for study and pleasure.

    Includes index.
    Summary: Gives instructions on how to acquire, care for, preserve, classify, display, and study animals, plants, rocks, and shells. Also includes ideas for projects, a bibliography, and a list of equipment and specimen suppliers.
    1. Biological specimens—Collection and preservation. 2. Geological specimens—Collection and preservation. 3. Natural history museums. 4. Museum techniques. [1. Biological specimens—Collection and preservation. 2. Geological specimens—Collection and preservation. 3. Natural history museums. 4. Museum techniques] I. Title.
QH61.B88 1984   069'.9508   84-12393
ISBN 0-668-06057-3 (Reference Text)
ISBN 0-668-06061-1 (Paper Edition)

Printed in the United States of America

10 9 8 7 6 5 4 3 2 1

To my two sons Kirby and Jerry,
who have been good companions
on many an adventurous collecting
hike into the out-of-doors

Contents

Museum Plans

Acknowledgments

In the course of preparing this book my most valued help came from Mr. Merton Hinshaw, Curator of the Natural History Museum at Pacific Grove, California. Mr. Hinshaw has developed many new and helpful techniques in museum work, as can be seen by anyone who visits his beautiful museum at Pacific Grove. Mr. Hinshaw was particularly helpful in the development of Chapter 7, on molds and models.

The molding supply company of Douglas and Sturgess also supplied me with useful information on molds and models. Mr. Douglas was kind enough to look over some of my work and give several helpful suggestions.

I am grateful to "Mom" and "Pop" Walton of Walton's Grizzly Lodge and Camp for Boys, Portola, California, for letting me work with their boys in developing several interesting nature exhibits during two summers I spent there.

Appreciation is due Dr. Carl D. Clarke for his kind permission to quote, on page 85 of this book, two resin–wax formulas from his book *Molding and Casting*.

Tools and Materials

Here are lists of some of the tools and materials you will need in using this book. Special materials and tools, as well as information on quantities, are described as they are needed throughout the book. You might want to photocopy these lists, indicate the quantities as you go along and use the lists as "shopping lists"—taking them with you to the hardware store or referring to them when you order supplies through the mail, for instance.

blotting paper
cardboard blotters
boards (for shelving, backings, etc.)
Masonite
plywood
glass
transparent plastic sheets

cheesecloth
cotton
ribbons
scissors
sewing needles
straight pins
thin wire

art gum eraser
cellophane tape
filing cards
labels
letter stencil sheets
masking tape
T-square, compass, and protractor

ballpoint and ink pens
black pencils
colored pencils
india ink

paints—transparent oil colors, watercolors, lacquer, enamel, poster
lacquer
shellac
varnish
paintbrushes
sandpaper
sealing compound
wood putty

formalin
isopropyl alcohol

glues—household cement, waterproof sealing cement, rubber cement, etc.
nails and screws
liquid plastic
modeling clay

papier-mâché
plaster of paris
resin–wax mixture
rubber molding material
rubber or latex mixture
soap
wax

cloth bags
collecting bags with compartments
jars—glass and plastic
small bottles and plastic vials
test tubes

forceps
geologist's pick
hammer
knapsack
notebook
10-power magnifying lens or
  low-power binocular microscope

hand or electric drill
saws
single-edge razor blades

1

Out-of-Doors Fun
Brought Indoors

It is a lot of fun to have your own nature museum, or to help build such a museum in a summer camp, school, club or other organization. Many more people would try to make such a museum if they understood how easy, inexpensive and interesting it is to do. Only your hands and your brains and a few materials such as ply-boards, glue, ink or paint, and a few specimens are needed to start. Probably the most important thing to begin with is deciding you want to make a museum that tells interesting stories about the world and its life, and so to do more than just show a group of collections.

In my book *The Amateur Naturalist's Handbook,* I have shown the amateur naturalist how to start in a simple, easy way with his nature collections and studies. In this book, my job is to show you how to take your collections and knowledge and make something as interesting as the beautiful displays of the out-of-door world you find in a fine natural history museum.

Believe it or not, you can take just a little corner of your room, or a school room or club room, and make that corner into such an exciting place that all your neighbors or club or school friends will want to see it and talk about it. You can bring your friends in and show them strange and interesting lessons about the world in which they live.

The secret is in learning how to make a good museum, so everyone who sees it will exclaim, "Say, you really have something here!" This book shows you how to plan and organize that museum, and how to make it.

I went to visit a young man recently who had a rock and mineral museum in his own room. It wasn't just an ordinary rock and mineral collection. He had glass cases he had made himself, and inside those cases he had most of the common rocks you can see any day when you take a long walk in the country. But there was nothing common about the way those rocks were exhibited. From each rock

1

long colored ribbons led in several directions. One red ribbon led to a picture above the rock that showed how the rock was made, a picture the young man had drawn himself.

"Dick," I asked, "how did you do it?"

"I looked up information about the rocks in geology books," said Dick, "and used their drawings to help me make my own drawings."

The other ribbons from the rock led to samples of the different kinds of minerals from which the rock was made, and printed next to each mineral was an interesting story about it. Here in one half of a bedroom was an exciting adventure in earth exploration. My friend Dick had a real natural history museum!

A nature museum can tell interesting stories not only about rocks and minerals, but about plants, animals, birds, insects, fossils and a thousand things you can find on every walk you take in the country. You don't need lots of money or lots of room. One little corner of your bedroom can be your personal nature museum. Of course, if you can have a whole room for your museum, so much the better.

One young woman I know made a living-room wall into a complete nature musuem. At first her mother and father objected, but when they saw what attractive and beautiful museum mounts she was preparing they were glad to let her take over the wall. There was a display of bird feathers at one place on the wall, arranged to show how the different colored feathers help the birds hide from enemies or win their mates. At another place was the complete history of a mountain lion's life from the time it was a cub until it was shot by a hunter. The story was told with pictures, lion and deer bones, teeth and fur. Hundreds who came into that room exclaimed over the beauty and value of the exhibits. Yet she had spent less than five dollars on them!

It is good to have glass cases to protect your specimens from handling and breakage. If you build your own cases, as you will be shown how to do in the next chapter, they won't cost more than a few dollars. But you do not need glass cases to start a museum. Shelves can be built out of old lumber or boxes and covered with oil-cloth or clean paper. Wall-display boards can be made with plywood or Basalite. A little hammering, a little gluing, a carefully planned display of correctly mounted and labeled specimens, and you are on your way to a fine nature museum.

The steps necessary to preparing a natural history museum are:

1. Decide you want to make a natural history museum.
2. Find out exactly how much room you can have for it.

3. Study this space carefully and decide what kinds of specimens and displays you want to use it for. (This you can know best after reading the suggestions in this book.)
4. Draw a diagram showing your plan for using the space. (The diagrams in Chapters 2 and 9 will help you with this, though these diagrams are more complete than the one you need to make.)
5. Start obtaining the specimens you need, following the directions in Chapter 3.
6. Classify your specimens as correctly as possible. (See Chapter 4.)
7. Mount and label your specimens correctly and attractively. (Chapter 5 gives you the details.)
8. Collect pictures or photographs that will go with your collections and help explain your museum displays. Some can be your own drawings or diagrams. In fact, because of our growing realization that specimens taken from life may be injurious to the balance of nature, or be forbidden by law in many places, photographs, paintings, drawings and models may be used just as attractively and with more justification for your museum exhibits. (Look in Chapters 6 and 8 for help.)
9. If you need to, build backgrounds in your museum cases with clay, papier-mâché, sand or wax. And make plaster, rubber or wax models of animals and plants. (See Chapters 7, 8 and 9.)
10. Arrange your whole museum in as interesting a way as you can. (You will find ideas to help you in Chapter 9.)
11. Keep developing and building your collections and displays into a museum that becomes more and more attractive, interesting and complete. You will find many ideas for doing this throughout the book. Your first work will naturally not be as good as what you do later, so replace your early work with better when you can.

2

Preparing Your Space for Museum Work

WHAT KINDS OF DISPLAYS?

The big question at first is: What kinds of displays do you want to make? Are you most interested in plants, insects, reptiles, mammals, birds, fossils, rocks or what? Look through the suggestions given in the pages of this book and the illustrations and diagrams of different kinds of displays and home museums. Soon you will begin to have ideas as to what kind you can have and want to have. Is it to be a miniature museum of natural history, with something from all the forms of life and matter discussed in Chapter 3? Or is it to be devoted principally to a few or to only one of those forms? Or something much more special which you have thought up for yourself?

If you can visit a good natural history museum near your home, their exhibits will also give you good ideas. If you use your own imagination besides, you can probably think up lots of interesting exhibits that have never been done before. (See also Appendix B for a list of books that will help you, and Chapter 11 for a final list of suggestions about museum displays and their making. Both are at the back of this book.)

DECIDING HOW TO USE YOUR SPACE FOR A MUSEUM

You must now look over what room you have and decide just how your space can be made into a museum. Then make a drawing or diagram like one of those in Plans 1, 2, 3, 4 or 5, only simpler, to show yourself just how you want to use that space. This is your blueprint of your museum.

NOTE: Plans 1, 2, 3 and 4 are shown in this chapter; Plan 5 is pictured in Chapter 9.

After you have decided just how you want to use the space, start building your shelves, cases and cabinets for display. You should know how much money you want to spend. If you are careful, and do all the building yourself, you need to spend very little.

HOW TO BUILD DISPLAY CASES AND CABINETS

There are five main ways to display your specimens, pictures, models and charts. These are:

1. *Mounting on boards.* To mount on boards is usually the simplest and cheapest method. The board you can use for mounting your display can be either Masonite or the more expensive besttile sheet, which is painted and lacquered. The Masonite can be painted or lacquered for a better finish. You can easily cut your board with a jigsaw into whatever shape will be most attractive when it is hung up on your wall. In Plan 2 you see one plywood board cut in the form of a half-circle. In Plan 3 a circular plywood board hangs above a fireplace. On this second board is displayed the life story of a sperm whale. The pictures of the display are glued or pinned to the plywood, and the specimens of bone, skin, etc., are either glued to the board or wired to it with thin wires.

    All such display boards should be carefully sandpapered before you put your mounts on them. Paint or varnish will also add to their appearance (Basalite boards need no painting). (Details on how to mount specimens and make models are given in Chapters 5 and 7.)

2. *Display shelves.* Ordinary bookshelves can be used for the display of specimens, or you can build your own shelves either in bookcase form or like the wall cases shown in Plan 1. Figure 1a gives details for building shelves. Be very careful to measure all distances between shelves so they are exactly even with the floor. Otherwise they will appear lopsided.

    Plan 2 shows shelves with specimens displayed upon them on one side in jars, and on the other side in glass display cases. Never use shelves merely to show rows of rocks or sea-

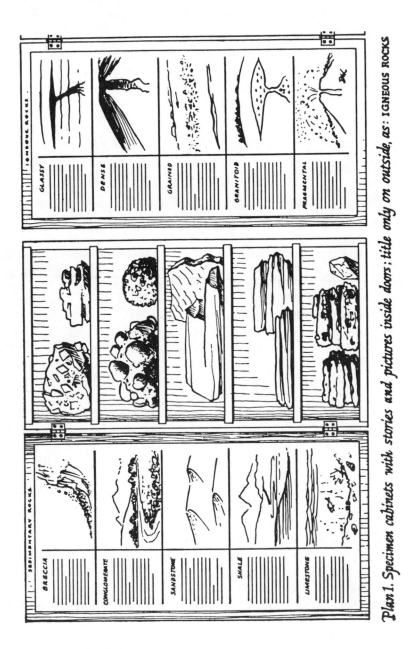

Plan 1. Specimen cabinets with stories and pictures inside doors; title only on outside, as: IGNEOUS ROCKS

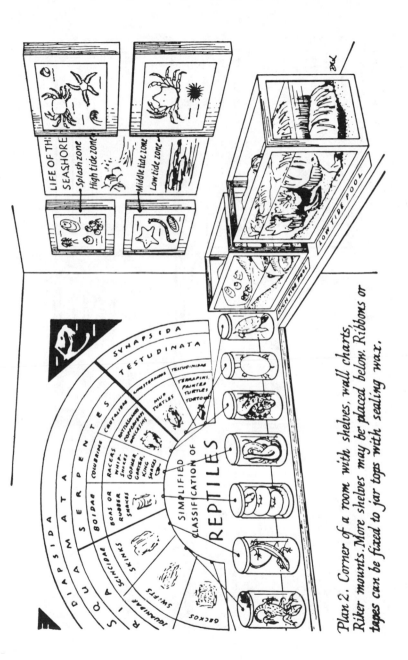

Plan 2. Corner of a room with shelves, wall charts, Riker mounts. More shelves may be placed below. Ribbons or tapes can be fixed to jar tops with sealing wax.

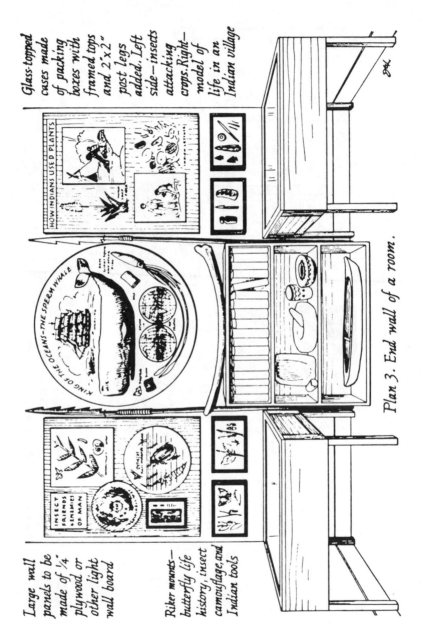

Plan 3. End wall of a room.

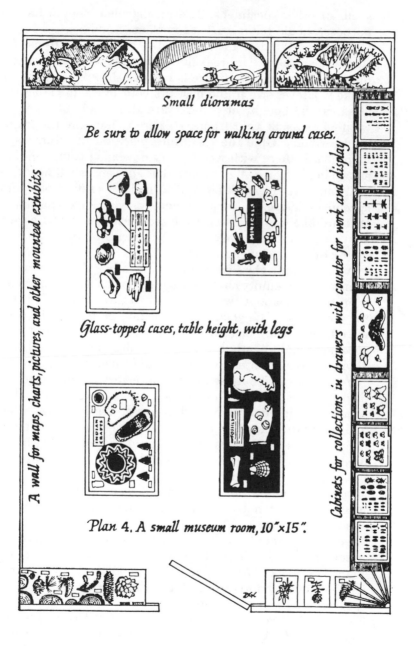

Small dioramas

Be sure to allow space for walking around cases.

A wall for maps, charts, pictures, and other mounted exhibits

Cabinets for collections in drawers with counter for work and display

Glass-topped cases, table height, with legs

Plan 4. A small museum room, 10"x15".

shells or other specimens. The arrangement should have a purpose, should tell a story, as in Plans 1 and 2.

3. *Glass cases.* Window glass is usually thick enough to use for small glass cases. Unbreakable transparent plastic sheets may also be used. The frame is built as shown in Figure 1b. Make whatever size frame best fits your museum. Then the glass can be bought at a hardware store and cut there to whatever sizes fit your frame. Be sure to measure the frame very carefully. Glue the glass into place on the frame and help hold it there with wood putty or sealing compound, as shown in the figure. A glass case that goes on a shelf next to a wall can have the back left out to make it easy to put your specimens inside. However, whenever you have specimens that are likely to be eaten by insect pests, or that are very valuable, you should have a tight wooden door on the back of your case (as is shown in Figure 1b).

A very simple glass case can be made like those shown in Plan 4. Put an empty shallow wooden box on short legs to lift it off the floor about two and a half to three feet. Cover the top with glass. The glass should fit into grooves so it won't fall off, and should be easy to lift up so that you can put your specimens underneath it. It is better still if the glass is tightly glued and sealed into a wooden-frame cover on hinges.

For an attractive museum it is necessary to sandpaper all display cases carefully until they are smooth. Then they should be painted or varnished to give protection to the wood and add to their appearance. Choose colors that do not glare.

Sometimes the insides of cases need to be lined with colored cloth or felt. This cloth should be clean and carefully pressed. Pick colors of cloth that contrast well with your specimens. Thus white minerals and rocks would go well on black cloth, but not on white cloth. Light green is often a good color to use.

Specimens should be arranged as attractively as possible inside these cases (see Chapter 9) and should tell a story. Plans 1, 2, 3, 4 and 5 will give you some ideas about what can be done, and Chapters 7, 8 and 9 will tell you how to make special mounts, models and dioramas.

4. *Mounted between glass and cotton in flat-box or picture-frame mounts.* How to make these mounts is described in Chapter 5. Examples of such mounts hung on the walls are shown in Plans 2 and 3.

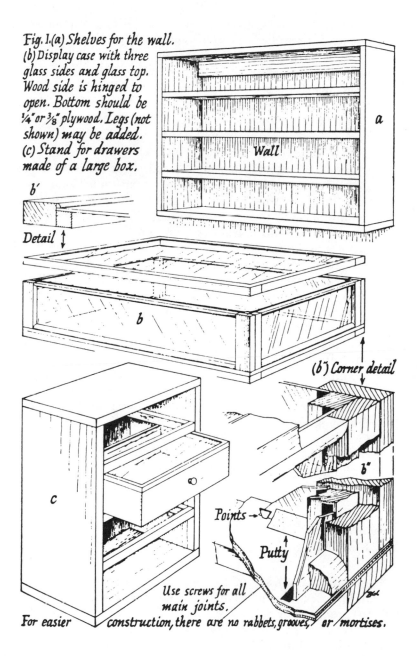

*Fig. 1. (a) Shelves for the wall.
(b) Display case with three
glass sides and glass top.
Wood side is hinged to
open. Bottom should be
¼" or ⅜" plywood. Legs (not
shown) may be added.
(c) Stand for drawers
made of a large box.*

b′

Detail ↕

a

Wall

b

(b′) Corner detail

b″

c

Points →

Putty

Use screws for all
main joints.

For easier   construction, there are no rabbets, grooves, or mortises.

5. *Cabinets.* Cabinets are too expensive for many people and do not lend themselves so well to storytelling as do the display methods already described. However, they do have one big advantage, and that is that a lot of material can be put into a small space. Figure 1c shows you how to build a simple cabinet of small drawers. Each drawer is covered with glass so that when you open one of your drawers to show a visitor part of your museum he will not be able to reach a finger in and break anything. The cabinet shown is of a size that works well with an insect collection. Shallower drawers can be used for rocks and minerals. (Glass covers are not usually necessary for plant, rock, seashell, fossil and mineral collections.)

Careful sandpapering and varnishing or painting are necessary to make your museum cabinet good-looking. Unless you are pretty handy with tools, you will probably not build a very good cabinet the first time you try it. Perhaps, however, if you take your time and are very careful to follow all directions, you may surprise yourself. Be sure to use a good grade of lumber and make the cabinet a size that fits exactly where and as you want it in your room.

You can keep more complete collections in cabinets than you can ever have on wall displays or in museum cases. To tell an interesting and instructive story the specimens in the drawers of the cabinet must be arranged according to a careful plan. With insects, for example, you should have one drawer showing butterflies, another moths, a third beetles, a fourth wasps and so on. More information and suggestions on this subject are given in Chapter 9. (Books that will help you with making cases and shelves are listed in the bibliography in Appendix B at the back of this book.)

HOW TO USE THE CORNER
OF A ROOM

There are many ways to use the corner of a room for a nature museum. Plan 2 shows one such way. The main thing to think about is how to arrange your displays so each tells a story, but they should also fit naturally and attractively into the corner.

The builder of the little museum shown in Plan 2 was interested in two things: reptiles and seashore life. One half of the room corner is given to each. On the left side he built a single shelf on which he placed jars of alcohol or formalin solution containing specimens of different kinds of reptiles.

He wanted to show the classification of reptiles, so he arranged his specimens in one order of their classification, with lizards on the left, snakes in the center and turtles on the right. Up above he hung a plywood board (or heavy paper) cut in the shape of a large half-circle. This he divided into sections showing main divisions of the reptile class and the characteristics in picture form of different kinds of reptiles. Then he strung colored ribbons from the specimen jars up to the proper sections on the chart. Thus the turtle jar was connected to the turtle section, the rattlesnake jar to the rattlesnake section, and so on. Pictures of reptiles in action were shown in the triangles above the chart. It should be noted here that photographs, paintings, drawings or models can always be used instead of actual specimens of living things, thus avoiding possible destruction of a life. See Chapters 6 and 7.

In the other half of his museum he hung four flat glass-covered boxes filled with cotton. These boxes contained specimens of animals and plants found in the different tide zones of the seashore. Ribbons from the box mounts led to a central chart where he showed in diagram form the nature of life on a rocky seashore. On the shelf below this chart he put two glass cases with models (see Chapter 7) of seashore life made out of rubber molding material or wax, and some actual specimens. The models showed how the animals and plants typical of the tide pools on the seashore appear in their natural surroundings.

Here then were two stories of wildlife told in such dramatic and interesting ways that at one glance you could learn more than from an hour's talk or lecture on the same subjects.

HOW TO USE A WALL OF A ROOM

Suppose you are given one wall of a room to make into a nature museum. You must study that wall carefully and make a diagram of what you want to do with it, a diagram somewhat like that shown in Plan 5. As in the illustration, plan a balanced display so that half of the wall balances the other half.

The museum maker who planned and built the displays shown in Plan 3 wanted to tell three stories: 1) the story of insect friends and enemies of man and how they act, 2) the life story of a sperm whale, and 3) the story of how the American Indians of his neighborhood once gathered and used wild plants.

In the first story he put two flat glass-covered mounts on the left side of the wall. One showed the life history of an insect enemy of man. The other showed how insects hide and protect themselves from their enemies. Above these mounts he placed a square plywood board (or heavy paper) on which he arranged pictures telling how some insects attack and destroy crops or even attack man himself, whereas other insects help man. Down below he had a glass case mounted on legs. In this case were examples of the work of insect enemies of man, and mounted specimens of insects that are friends of man were also shown doing their useful work.

In the middle of the wall above the fireplace the museum maker told the story of the life of a sperm whale, using a large circular plywood board. This he did mainly with pictures showing different events in the whale's life. But also there were glued or wired to the board pieces of whale skin, a whale tooth, and parts of whale bone. Down on the mantel above the fireplace was a larger whale bone, and to either side were two harpoons. These last gave a feeling of extra interest and reality to the story of the whale.

On the right-hand side of the wall appeared the story of how a neighborhood tribe of American Indians used wild plants. On a square plywood board (or cardboard) were pictures of the Indians using plants, and mounted specimens of these plants. Down below were two glass-covered cotton-filled boxes showing the tools they used in gathering the plants or in making use of them. Still lower was a glass museum case in which the museum maker used papier-mâché, modeling clay, and wax and plaster casts (see Chapters 7 and 9) to make a model of life in an Indian village. He showed in this village how the Indians used the wild plants they brought in from the surrounding country.

Some of these stories are simpler and easier to show in your museum than others. But even the simple stories are interesting.

HOW TO MAKE A MUSEUM
IN A SMALL ROOM

Perhaps you are a lucky person with a whole room you can turn into a nature museum. Or possibly you are helping build a nature museum at a camp, school or clubhouse. Plan 4 gives suggestions about how to use an entire room. Each wall, of course, can be made to tell various stories such as those shown in Plans 2 and 3. The glass-covered cases that stand in the center of the room should be placed so that visitors can walk around them and look from all sides at the things displayed. These display cases should also tell stories. You could arrange your mineral specimens to show the gradation from hard to soft minerals or to show some of the valuable uses of various minerals. You could fix your rock specimens so they would be classified as to how they were formed. You could fix your Indian relics to tell a story in the history of a certain tribe. And so on.

Though there are hundreds of ways to arrange your room to make an attractive museum, there are only a few simple rules to follow. These are good rules for any size museum:

- Don't clutter the room with so many specimens that it becomes confusing to visitors. Make it simple and easy to understand.
- Make every specimen take part in the telling of some story.
- Keep your museum neat and clean. Dust it frequently and keep all your specimens in correct order.
- Keep out pests that eat specimens by sprinkling mothball flakes or paradichloride of benzene crystals in your cases. Also regularly inspect your specimens and kill all pests you find. If many pests appear, you may have to close the room and fumigate it with a powerful insect killer.
- When the room is not in use keep out direct sunlight, as the light causes both pictures and specimens to fade.
- Be sure that your cases and display mounts are securely put together and strongly fastened to either the floor or the wall so that they will not be easily jarred loose.

KEEP TRYING TO IMPROVE

When you have a nature museum you take on a new name. You become a *curator*. A curator is a man or woman who looks after a museum. A real curator has to have one very necessary quality. He or she always keeps trying to improve the museum. The following pages will give you many suggestions about how to improve yours.

3

Obtaining Specimens

Not too many years ago obtaining specimens—whether they were rocks, plants or animals—was relatively simple. You went to where the rocks or plants or animals were and collected them, doing whatever was necessary to obtain your specimen: digging up rocks, cutting branches off trees, shooting mammals. Today obtaining specimens is very different, and should be very different.

Some beautiful parts of the earth and many beautiful and interesting creatures have been threatened by pollution and other forms of destruction—including overcollecting. Some animals have become extinct, others nearly so. We need to reverse the terrible trend of destruction and move our earth "back on the beauty path," as the Navahos say. Instead of destroying, we need to add to and beautify life.

The best way to contribute your share is to avoid collecting altogether. You can take pictures, make models, and draw and paint the rocks, plants and mammals you need for your museum. With skill you will be able to replicate most any organism or object with great realism. Just think how realistic are the wax figures in a wax museum. Why, they seem more lifelike than real people! If you do need specimens, you can obtain them from companies that specialize in supplying them. Appendix C lists many of these companies, from which you can order anything from slides of protozoa to skeletons of monkeys; rocks and minerals; plants; and virtually anything else you might need for your museum. Plants, of course, can be purchased from garden shops and florists; many rock shops sell shells and rocks; and taxidermists sell preserved animals.

However, if you are like most people, you probably will collect some of the specimens you want anyway. This chapter can show you how to collect properly, whether you are collecting only to photograph, paint, model, or draw a creature or object and then return it to where you found it, or whether you are collecting in order to take home something to preserve or mount and then add to your museum display.

If you do collect, try to be selective and careful, taking only what you absolutely need. Treat living creatures with great respect. And leave the collection site the way you found it (if you dug a hole to get a rock, fill the hole when you're through; if you turned up a stone to look for sow bugs, put the stone back when you're through). Or better yet, leave the site more unspoiled than you found it (it is a great thrill to visit an area such as a campground and leave no traces of your being there when you leave).

THE COLLECTING SPIRIT

When the world brightens up with a beautiful morning and the air has a tang like wine, that is a day for you to go collecting. Hiking over the hills or through the valleys, hunting along the seashore or the marshes, you see deep into the secrets of the wild. You see adventure tales in the delicate footprints of the sandpipers by the pond, or the hidden chrysalises of butterflies under the old water tower. From your wanderings you bring back bits of what you have seen: interesting insects, some odd stones, some plaster casts of tracks you have found in the sand. From all these your busy hands build things of beauty and interest in your home, displays that tell a story of pebbles washed from hills where they were once part of the fiery heart of the earth, or the wonderful life story of an insect, or the meaning of footprints on the ground.

NOTE TAKING

When you are hiking over the hills looking for things to use in making an interesting museum display, be sure to take a notebook. In this notebook you can write down ideas you may get about a planned exhibit. If you have already planned an exhibit and are collecting things for it, then you must take notes on what you collect. It is from these notes that you build interesting parts of your story.

Suppose you uncover a termite nest in an old log, and you are going to make a museum display telling the story of termites. Then you would take notes something like these:

May 24, 1984, Phoenix, Arizona; five miles west of town along Highway 80. Log beside road was full of termites, probably the long-nosed termite, *Constrictotermes tenuirostris (Desneux)*. The workers have large brown heads and white bodies about ⅜ inch long. The soldiers or *nasuti* are only a little larger and have black heads from which emerge what look like long noses or tubes. They have brown bodies. The winged males and females are yellowish brown and covered with very short yellowish hair. They are about ¾ inch long.

As soon as I cut open one of the earthen tunnels along one side of the log, the soldier termites or *nasuti* with their "squirt-gun" heads appeared. They pointed their nozzles outward. When I put an ant among them they immediately squirted him with a fluid that made him run away in a great hurry. I then saw a strange thing. When the pale-colored workers brought up pieces of dirt to fix the broken tunnel, the squirt-gun soldiers cemented the dirt together with the stuff from their guns! The winged males and females were running excitedly through the tunnel. Some came outside and flew off, so it must be the mating season when new colonies are started.

A very interesting part of a museum display would be to show large models of these squirt-gun soldiers fighting and working. It could be done by hand-modeling wax or possibly using clay.

Actual observations like this written on the spot help you very much in planning your museum displays. Most people forget many things that they have watched unless they carefully write down what they see.

COLLECTING ROCKS AND MINERALS

The main tool needed in collecting rocks and minerals is a geologist's pick. This can be bought or ordered at a hardware store. An ordinary hammer can be used as a substitute, but the pointed end of the pick makes it a handier tool. The geologist's pick or the hammer is used for breaking open rock and mineral specimens or breaking a piece off a larger rock. Often astonishing things are found inside broken rocks. For example, some round brown rocks that look good for nothing may be broken open and show you beautiful and valuable agates or other pretty minerals. These round rocks are called geodes.

On a rock and mineral collecting trip it is best to carry with you a small knapsack for carrying your specimens. About 2 inches in diameter is a good size for a specimen, so break pieces of about this size. Of course smaller sizes can be used too. Another useful thing to carry is a roll of white adhesive tape. Take a small square piece of adhesive tape and stick it on each specimen. Mark a different number on each specimen on this piece of tape. In your notebook write where each specimen has been found, as:

Rocks collected January 24, 1984.

55. Red rock in stream bed five miles east of Pescadero, California. Near road to Portola State Park. Well rounded by water.

56. From old mine on Stevens Creek Road, two miles above Stevens Creek Dam, Santa Clara County, California. Part of a streak of reddish-brown rock in back of shaft.

Keeping notes on where specimens have been found is extremely important for at least two reasons. One is that you may, on careful study, find that the rock or mineral you found is valuable or could lead to something valuable. If you then have no notes on your specimen, you will often not know where to go to find the same thing again. It is an absolute truth that great fortunes have been lost because of exactly this kind of carelessness. The second reason is that your collection can have value to the scientific geologist only if the location from which each specimen comes is correctly given. Knowing locations is what helps him map and understand the distribution of rocks and minerals in the earth's surface. Your collection might give him a key to this valuable understanding. It would certainly be foolish to lose such a key because of forgetting to take notes!

There are many good places to look for rocks and minerals. The following are suggested: 1) train-track and road cuts through hills and mountain sides; 2) canyons which swift streams have cut, exposing fresh rock; 3) mines and quarries; 4) landslides; and 5) lake and ocean shores where stones have been thrown by the waves. Search these places and others where fresh rock is exposed and you may find many treasures. The wonderful thing is that each year the action of wind, water and man lays bare further secrets of the earth to the eye of the collector.

COLLECTING SOILS, CHEMICALS, ETC.

For the collecting of soils and similar specimens you had best carry with you small glass or plastic vials or bottles. In these small bottles place samples of the soil you have found. Each bottle should be numbered, and in your notebook opposite each number describe where you found the specimen, as shown above for rocks.

Many interesting experiments can be done with soils. These experiments can be illustrated in your museum display by charts, diagrams, pictures and actual specimens. You can test soils for how much water they take in, for which kinds of plants grow best in them, for ways they can be used as building materials (such as adobe, cement, etc.), for their ability to hold water at the surface, and so on.

A collection of chemicals in bottles would go with a museum display showing how these chemicals are used by man. You can obtain chemicals from mines, from many industrial plants (particularly chemical plants), from college laboratories and from your neighborhood drugstore. Be careful not to taste any that may be poisonous, and wash your hands after using.

COLLECTING PLANTS

Plants should be collected for specimens only when you know there are large numbers of that particular plant about, or if your local botanical department at a college or university tells you a certain plant is numerous enough to be collected.

One of the main troubles with collecting plants is their wilting. To classify or name a plant it is best to have it in fresh condition. But you seldom have time on a collecting hike to take a book along and classify each plant as you find it.

To bring plants home in fairly fresh condition for classifying them, carry them in a tin vasculum (such as is shown in Figure 2). Or you can carry with you in your knapsack a cardboard box full of wet sheets of newspaper and lay each plant between separate sheets. Put in a slip of paper with each plant and write on the slip a number, where you found the plant, and the date. Use a trowel to get roots as well as stems, leaves, and flowers or fruits of each plant.

WARNING: Make sure you do not choose plants protected by law, and never remove plants unless you can leave several untouched nearby.

At the same time that you bring home plants to be classified, collect duplicates or other examples of these same plants to be pressed in your plant press. This press (as shown in Figure 2) is made of two plywood boards through which are bored holes to let in air. Between the boards are many layers of newspaper, and the press is made to cover completely an ordinary folded newspaper sheet. Around the boards are buckled two straps which can be pulled tight to press the plants. Several good specimens of a plant are placed inside the single folded sheet of a newspaper with the number of the

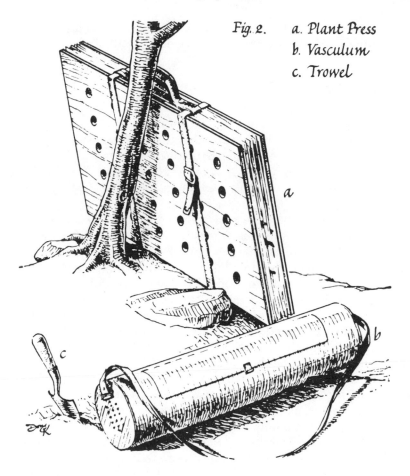

Fig. 2. a. Plant Press
b. Vasculum
c. Trowel

plant (the same number that is kept with the fresh specimen of the same plant), the date collected and the place all written on one corner of the paper. This folded sheet is then covered on both sides by layers consisting of twelve newspaper sheets each. Beyond these layers on either side, other groups of plant specimens can be placed in other single folded sheets.

Instead of the layers of newspaper sheets between plants you can use heavy cardboard blotters. These can usually be bought from large paper companies. The important thing to remember about plant pressing is to change the papers or blotters once a day for five or six days, putting in fresh dry ones each day. Dry out the old blotters or papers in the sun or near a heater. Using fresh paper or blotters each day helps dry out the plants until they are ready for permanent mounting (see Chapter 5). Seaweeds need a special type of pressing and mounting that is described in Chapter 5.

COLLECTING FOSSILS

Fossils are ancient animals and plants that through long ages have gradually turned into rock. Ask at your nearest university in the geology or paleontology department for information about local fossils and where they can be found. Remember that fossils are sometimes extremely valuable to science, so do not destroy any you find.

Because of this possible great value, it is essential that you write careful notes about where each fossil is found, identifying the exact location and detailing the types of rocks found there. These notes must then be transferred to a label kept with the fossil in your museum so that all the information is kept together and so can be used by a paleontologist to understand the history of your specimen, its value and the meaning of the locality where it was found. He can then add the specimen data to his store of scientific knowledge of our earth and make it a vital part of the accumulation of scientific facts about the earth, probably writing about it in a book. If the species actually is a newly discovered one, unknown to science, then your name may be used to name the species—a great honor!

Fossils are usually found inside rocks. Sometimes, if certain rocks are broken up, amazing fossils are found inside them. In the Badlands of South Dakota my wife and I once found the backbone and leg of an ancient horse, possibly more than ten million years old. In the hills back of Berkeley, California, I found the fossil trunks of ancient willow trees. In the hills behind Los Altos, California, we have found leaves and twigs in a little creek being almost fossilized before our eyes. The water was so full of lime that layers of limestone were blanketing the leaves and twigs, often enough to cover them with rock within a year.

You need a geologist's pick or similar tool to pick out fossils from the rock. Great care must be used, as fossils are often very fragile. In the mountains of British Columbia, where we found fossils of trilobites, ancient sea animals more than three hundred million years old, we had to pick for hours to get some of them out of the rock. In some cases we made plaster molds of what we found (see Chapter 7). From these plaster molds (or negatives), plaster, rubber or wax models (or positives) can be made.

All fossils you find should be carefully labeled and numbered. Write down the exact place and time you found them and describe the condition and appearance of the neighboring rock. This will help geologists who see your collection figure out what kind of rock formation the fossils were found in. They may be able to tell you the age of the rock. Sometimes from the fossils they can tell whether there are pools of oil lying under the rock.

COLLECTING SEASHORE LIFE

The rocky shores of the sea are far more fruitful of life than the sandy beaches. On the sand beaches and the mud flats of the bays most things lie buried under the surface and must be dug for with a small shovel. On the rocky beaches you hunt through the tide pools with a small dip net. You look under the piles of seaweed, turn over the rocks and dig in the sand and mud below the rocks, uncovering thousands of living things.

Because many tidal areas are so densely populated with these creatures, many people feel it won't hurt to take home a crab, a starfish or a bucketful of mussels. But in truth so many people have collected specimens and animals—for various purposes—that many beaches and tide pools have been stripped of a great deal of their beautiful and interesting life. In fact, most places have strict laws against such collecting. Therefore, collecting seashore life, unless done in conjunction with an institution such as a museum or university, should simply not be done. You will have to content yourself with modeling, photography, drawing and painting the specimens you want (see Chapters 6 and 8).

In order to do this you may, however, have to collect specimens temporarily so that you can study and replicate them. *Be sure to keep specimens wet so they won't dry out and die.* You can temporarily keep them in a bucket of sea water. Another possibility is to bring an aquarium down to the seashore, fill it with sea water, and put your specimens into the aquarium, with a background of rocks, pebbles, seaweed, driftwood and so forth. You can then do your photographing, modeling, etc. Make sure you change the water in the bucket or aquarium at least every two or three hours. Always return specimens to exactly the same places you found them. For example, if you overturned a rock and picked up a crab, put the crab back in the spot where the rock was and place the rock back on top (being careful not to crush the crab, of course!).

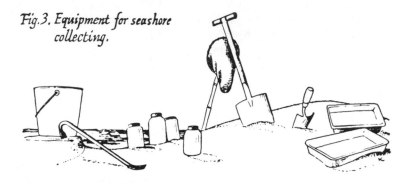

Fig.3. Equipment for seashore collecting.

Figure 3 shows some of the tools needed in collecting at the seashore. The small shovel is used mostly in the sand and in the bay mud flats. The trowel is useful everywhere, for digging and for prying. In the bucket you can put the specimens you find and bring them back to the beach to be sorted over. The small steel pry is useful for prying the larger shellfish off the rocks and for turning over the rocks. The shallow trays (best if made of white enamelware) are for putting specimens into from the buckets. In these trays you may sort them out and classify them (see next chapter).

Rubber hip boots are very useful in seashore collecting. But, if you don't mind too much getting wet, you will find a pair of old tennis shoes good enough. Always remember that the sea can be dangerous. When collecting below cliffs, it is wise to have a long rope attached to you and to somebody or a rock or stake on land. People have been washed into the sea and drowned by unexpectedly big waves, especially on the more open coasts. If the place where you are collecting is protected by offshore rocks or islets, it is not so dangerous. If you see a big wave coming, don't run for shore unless you have plenty of time. Better to crouch or lie down and hang onto a rock. You will get wet, but not knocked off and sucked under as might otherwise be possible. I learned this lesson well one day when caught in a great tidal wave at Punta Burica on the Pacific coast of Costa Rica.

The most numerous life on the shore is on the more protected coasts where the surf is not so powerful. Here creatures swarm everywhere. There are rarely any really dangerous animals, though the stinging white sponge and some of the big crabs can make you very uncomfortable. Most crabs when grabbed about the middle of the body cannot pinch you. An exception is a large kelp crab (body shaped like an ax head). When he grabs for you, better let him go!

Many things that look like plants are actually animals. The hydroids, for example, often look like bunches of feathers or ferns. The sea anemones look like flowers.

The seashore is divided into four zones: 1) the *splash zone,* where only the highest waves reach; 2) the *high tide zone,* where the highest barnacles and mussels live; 3) the *middle tide zone,* where life really begins to get thick; and 4) the *low tide zone,* where every inch of space seems covered with living things and the large round cancer crabs haunt the tide pools. As you watch the ebb and flow of the tide you will begin to see the range of these different zones of life. Look in your local newspaper or go to your local sporting goods store for information on when there are good low tides. These are called minus tides and are marked with a –0.3 or –0.7 in the tide tables found in most newspapers. They are good times to collect and to study the seashore life.

In your notebook and on your labels mark down the tide zones where your different specimens came from. Also mark whether they were found on top of the rocks, on the sides of the rocks, hidden under the seaweed, or under the rocks. Each kind of animal has to find the place that best suits it to live. This is all part of the fascinating story of the sea, and can be put into many beautiful and interesting museum displays.

Information on how to make models of the many strange creatures of the sea can be found in Chapter 7.

COLLECTING INSECTS AND SIMILAR CREATURES

Where to Look for Insects and Spiders

Many people miss small creatures that are right under their noses because they don't know where to look. Most insects have hiding places, and many disguise themselves to look like something else. The stick insects, for example, look like small dead twigs of bushes or trees.

While collecting insects (especially the more successful ones) is unlikely to cut down their numbers seriously—and some insects are so harmful that the more you collect the better—we cannot look at all insects with the same eyes, seeing them all as enemies of the human race. You should not collect the kinds of extremely beautiful butterflies and beetles that are threatened with extinction as a result of overcollection. Nor should you collect the many kinds of insects that are allies of mankind in fighting insect pests: allies such as the lacewings, ladybug beetles, and many wasplike parasites (which control the numbers of harmful caterpillars and locusts). Treat such insects with great respect. Learn to distinguish allies from pests and to distinguish the rare and beautiful insects. Using a camera, modeling materials or drawing and painting materials is a worthwhile way to "collect" specimens for your museum and indeed may require more ingenuity than using a net!

Should you wish or need to collect and preserve insects, the following information tells you just how to do it.

Under and on bark, under leaves, under stones and boards, and in the hearts of flowers are hiding places of insects. Turn over boards, logs and rocks (always turning them back for new hiders). Look under loose bark, search in the leaves, shake flowers into jars—these are some of the things to do to find insects. Butterflies love to come to damp places on a road, especially if a little honey or syrup is spilled there.

Remember that most insects and spiders are completely harmless. Only a few of the larger spiders, including particularly the black widow, are able to hurt people. Also, large beetles can bite hard, a few large bugs can pierce fingers with their beaklike mouths, most ants have acid bites, and wasps and bees can sting. Even these creatures are all easily handled with forceps and many of them even with bare fingers once you have had experience with them and overcome fear.

Tools for Collecting Insects and How to Use Them

Figure 4 shows some of the many tools used for collecting insects. The insect net (4a) is probably the most important. An old broom handle, some stiff wire, some tape and a piece of bobbinet, green voile, or cheesecloth cut in a U-shaped pattern and sewn on the wire frame makes the net. Forceps (4b) are important for picking up insects, especially the stinging kinds. Get a copper tube, pinch the end and solder a handle on the tube, so the forceps can be carried on the belt. A trowel is useful for digging in the dirt or under bark. A small hand ax can be used to cut away dead bark.

In using an insect net on a butterfly or other insect in flight, it is important to come up behind the creature with a swift motion and net it. Butterflies and moths may be quickly killed by pinching them

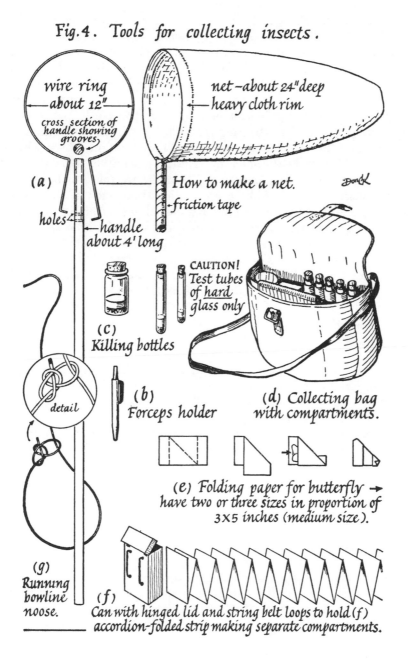

Fig.4. Tools for collecting insects.

wire ring about 12"

cross section of handle showing grooves

net — about 24" deep — heavy cloth rim

(a)

How to make a net.

holes

handle about 4' long

friction tape

CAUTION! Test tubes of *hard* glass only

(c) Killing bottles

(b) Forceps holder

(d) Collecting bag with compartments.

detail

(e) Folding paper for butterfly → have two or three sizes in proportion of 3×5 inches (medium size).

(g) Running bowline noose.

(f) Can with hinged lid and string belt loops to hold (f) accordion-folded strip making separate compartments.

sharply on the chest or thorax while the wings are folded over the back in the net. Do not touch the wings, or you will ruin the specimen by rubbing off the scales. It is wise to handle insects as little as possible to avoid breakage. To kill insects other than butterflies and moths, drop them into poison jars (see below).

A beating net is made in the same way as the usual insect net except that the wire is heavier and so is the cloth material. The beating net is used for beating through light brush and among tree branches. Many creatures are knocked loose and into the net by this method. All may be dumped into a large poison jar. A beating cloth can be made by spreading out a 3-foot-square piece of heavy cloth and placing two sticks like a cross with their ends in each corner. Cloth pockets are then sewn over the stick ends to hold them there and the sticks are tied together in the middle. A hole is drilled in the end of another stick about 4 feet long and a stout string is used to run through this hole and tie the stick tightly to the middle of the cross sticks. This beating cloth is held under a bush, which is beaten with a stick until hidden insects fall onto the cloth to be collected.

Poison Jars

Potassium cyanide or sodium cyanide has long been used in poison jars for insects, but these chemicals are so deadly that I recommend using ethyl acetate, which is much safer and can usually be obtained at your local drugstore.

Start off by buying a pint of the ethyl acetate. Fill the bottom of a pint or quart jar with about an inch of plaster of paris mixed with water to make a thick cream (mix in a crockery bowl). Allow this to harden and then bake in a low oven (about 105° F, 41° C) until all moisture is gone from the plaster. Now pour about a half inch or more of ethyl acetate on top of the dry plaster and allow the jar to sit with its cover on for a couple of days. The plaster absorbs most of the ethyl acetate in this time, and what is left can be poured off. Now place a circular piece of blotting paper (better two or three pieces) over the plaster of paris. This takes up any extra moisture. This jar will kill most insects (though large beetles may take a long time). It will last for about a year. If ethyl acetate gets on any insect in the jar, the liquid should be washed off with a little ether on the tip of a brush.

Several different poison jars should be carried on a collecting trip, so that different kinds of insects may be put in different jars (see Figure 4d). Large beetles, for example, would ruin delicate flies if put in the same jar.

Other Helps in Insect Collecting

After death, insects may be put in transparent paper envelopes or folded envelopes (such as those shown in Figure 4e) and carried in a shirt pocket or a carrying bag. Butterflies may be put in such a carrying box as is shown in Figure 4f. A long strip of paper is made and this is folded to fit into the box. Mark envelopes with the date and place of capture of the specimens. Keep notes, too, in your notebook.

Insects should be mounted, if possible, within one day after they die (see Chapter 5). Otherwise they become stiff and hard and have to be relaxed all over again.

Water insects need a special water net for collecting. A good stiff rim is needed on this net and the netting material must stand constant dipping in water. Bobbinet is good.

Figure 5 shows a light trap such as is used for collecting night insects, particularly moths. The poison jar at the bottom of the trap is taken off in the morning and the insects dumped out on a sheet of white paper. Another good way to collect night insects is to spread a

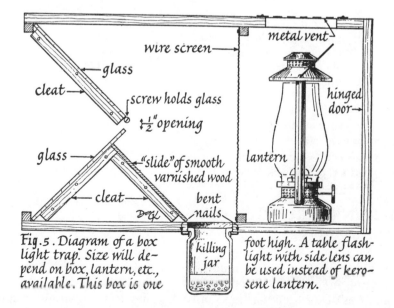

Fig. 5. Diagram of a box light trap. Size will depend on box, lantern, etc., available. This box is one foot high. A table flashlight with side lens can be used instead of kerosene lantern.

sheet against a wall facing brushland or forest on a dark and hot summer night. Place a Coleman lantern in front of the sheet so that its bright light will attract hundreds of insects to the white surface. Use two or three poison jars, putting the more delicate insects into one jar and the tougher ones into another.

A still different way to catch night insects is to mix up and boil together some molasses, beer and rotten apples. This mixture can be painted on the bark of trees or on strips of cloth hung from trees. Come around at night with a bright flashlight to these bait trees and you will find many interesting insects attracted to the sweets.

Spiders and the soft-bodied larvae of insects should be collected in small bottles of undenatured alcohol, which can be about 70 percent, but must later be increased by stages to 80 or 90 percent or even more, depending on the softness of the creature's body. These bottles are labeled on the spot with the date and place of collection. The name may be added later if you can find it. It may be difficult for you to get alcohol. A 10 percent formalin solution (one part of formalin to ten parts of water) may be used, but it makes spiders very brittle.

A possible answer to this problem is to explain to your druggist that you need a good solution for preserving delicate insects, and have him make up the following:

Ingredient	*Proportion* (*in cubic centimeters*)
Acetic acid (33 percent)	10 cc.
Hydrargyri perchloride (liquid)	10 cc.
Glycerine	10 cc.
Alcohol (90 percent)	80 cc.
Distilled water	50 cc.

This is the same solution used by scientists to preserve soft-bodied creatures under cover glasses on microscopic slides. It keeps them in good condition for many years.

Caterpillars can be taken home while they are still fresh and mounted by being blown with hot air (see Chapter 5).

OBTAINING REPTILES AND AMPHIBIANS

Since reptiles and amphibians are almost universally allies of mankind, helping to keep down the numbers of insect and rodent pests, I advise collecting them only in order to photograph, model, draw or paint them for your museum, and then releasing them. Even the poisonous snakes, such as rattlesnakes, are useful in controlling these pests and should be killed only around houses, where they could be dangerous to children. Thus, information will be provided on skinning a snake.

Reptiles and amphibians may be collected in cloth bags of different sizes (see Figure 6a). Each bag has a drawstring for tying it shut sewn onto the upper end of the bag. Small flour and sugar sacks are good bags to use. Carry the bags in your pocket or in your knapsack or collecting bag. A few small reptiles and amphibians may be put into one bag. Amphibians must be kept damp or they will soon dry out and shrivel up.

In the United States there are only four kinds of really dangerous snakes and one dangerous lizard (these are shown in Figure 6b). There are no dangerous salamanders, frogs or toads. Until you become an expert with reptiles it is wise not to collect or handle poisonous kinds. The expert, of course, catches them by pinning down their heads and seizing them quickly by the neck. He carries them in strong bags kept in a leather or plastic carrying case through which they cannot strike. Don't think you are an expert until you have had several years' experience with reptiles and have worked with a trained naturalist who has taught you the tricks.

Figure 6 shows you some of the tools and snares used for collecting reptiles and amphibians. Lizards, snakes and salamanders may also be caught in insect nets such as the one shown in Figure 4a. A water net is used to catch salamanders, frogs and toads in ponds and streams. The noose on the end of a long pole (shown in Figure 4g) is particularly useful for catching lizards, but may also be used for collecting snakes. Be sure to use a good grade of fish line and form the noose with a bowline knot. You sneak up on a resting lizard or snake and slowly slip the noose over his head. Once over, suddenly jerk it tight and haul the animal in as you do when catching a fish. The specimen is then untied and placed in the reptile bag.

The can trap shown in Figure 6c is excellent for catching small lizards and snakes. Bury the can to its top in places where the animals have been seen. Cover the top with a board placed on stones. Come to look every few hours and take out any specimens caught. The wire trap (6d) is harder to make, but is useful especially in brushy country and along streams. Snakes in particular wander into such traps while on their nightly journeys.

Many reptiles and amphibians hide under logs and boards. After such hiding places are turned over and specimens collected, always

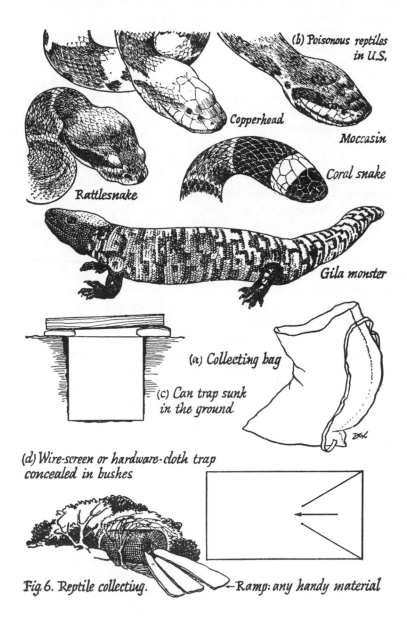

(b) *Poisonous reptiles in U.S.*

Copperhead

Moccasin

Coral snake

Rattlesnake

Gila monster

(a) *Collecting bag*

(c) *Can trap sunk in the ground*

(d) *Wire-screen or hardware-cloth trap concealed in bushes*

Fig. 6. Reptile collecting.   *Ramp: any handy material*

be sure to turn them back in place. They will make good hiding places for new animals. Many salamanders hide under bark, in rotten wood and even in the leaf-filled crotches of large trees. Also look under leaf mold. Be ready to grab any animal quickly before it can recover from its surprise and escape.

The wire-screen trap suggested for snakes (see Figure 6d) is also good for turtles in ponds and streams. Wire the trap to the bottom with long wires attached to rocks. Look in the trap at least once a day. Be extremely careful about snapping turtles. The bite of these fierce reptiles can be very painful. Most other inland turtles and tortoises are comparatively harmless, though it is wise to keep your fingers away from their mouths. Remember, all need to have air they can reach when trapped.

COLLECTING MAMMALS

Mammals are usually haired animals like the dog and cat. Mammals may be trapped or shot to obtain their skins and skeletons. However, you must be careful to obey the game laws of your state. The beginning museum maker would be wise to leave mammals alone for a while, except for such comparatively simple jobs as collecting specimens of their bones, fur, teeth, tracks, pictures of them, and so forth. The reason for this is that learning how to mount mammals in attractive museum groups takes a lot of careful training and experience. Until you are prepared to take such training there is not much use in killing mammals for your museum, as this will probably be quite wasteful.

Skeletons, horns, bits of fur and teeth of mammals killed in the wild may be found on your hikes. If you collect any of these, do a careful job. Put each thing you find in a numbered or labeled bag. Regular grocery bags will do, using large bags for whole skeletons. If your bags are numbered, then put in your notebook under "Mammal Collections" the numbers and opposite each number the date collected, the place and anything else of interest. For example, you may find signs of a struggle and the tracks of a mountain lion near a deer skeleton. Be sure to tell about this in your notes because the information may be very useful in planning your exhibit.

WARNING: Do not pick up dead rodents. They may be diseased.

Bones should be cleaned by boiling them in water with a little bleach added. Scrape off dirt and meat.

COLLECTING BIRDS

Almost all birds are protected by law, and this is because nearly all birds are more useful than they are harmful. Most birds eat harmful insects and some, such as owls, hawks and eagles, kill and eat harmful rodents. Since even picking up and skinning a dead bird you find may get you in trouble with the law, you should contact your local game warden if you are interested in obtaining birds for your museum. It is probably safe, however, to pick up bones and feathers that you find and learn their identity from studying books or talking to a biologist or naturalist.

Bones, feathers and similar things are collected in the same way as has already been described for mammal bones and fur. One of the most interesting collections can be made by finding the disgorged and dried pellets of hawks and owls. These pellets, usually dropped by the birds at the feet of trees and cliffs where they have their nests, contain the bones and fur of animals they have killed. By sorting these out and studying them carefully you can see exactly what the birds have been feeding on.

Old bird nests should be collected rather than new ones. You have to either observe birds around their nests or study books about nests in order to recognize kinds of bird nests. Handle nests carefully, as they break easily. By wrapping a newspaper around a nest and putting both in a paper or cloth bag, you help prevent breakage. Each nest should have a slip of paper with it telling where it was collected and the nature of its surroundings. Never collect birds' eggs unless they have rolled out of nests and are still intact and without interest to the birds. You can blow the contents out of such eggs by breaking a tiny hole in each end, then inserting a small glass or plastic tube and blowing through it. Try to make sure, without disturbing the birds in their nests, what kind of bird each such egg came from, and then place it, labeled with the name, date and habitat as well as location, in an old nest you have collected that is no longer in use. Arranged attractively in your museum, such a nest will add significantly to your display.

NOTE: How to study wild animals, plants, rocks, minerals, fossils and the weather is described in detail in *The Amateur Naturalist's Handbook*. Such study helps in planning museum exhibits.

STORING COLLECTIONS

Collecting specimens leads first to classifying what you have collected and then to mounting and displaying your collections in your museum (see Chapters 5, 7 and 9). But sometimes you cannot classify and mount your specimens right away, and then they must be stored. Above all try to keep plant and animal specimens in a dry place, unless they are in airtight jars. Insects will soon mold if kept in wet places. Mold can be fought by crystals of carbolic acid kept in the boxes or drawers where the specimens are stored.

Many collections of animals are ruined by insects' eating them. If you can, keep such collections in airtight boxes and even in these boxes keep mothball flakes or crystals of paradichloride of benzene. In any case keep plentiful supplies of these flakes and crystals scattered through all your collections to repel pests. Look at your collections often to make sure pests are not getting into them. If you find pests eating your collections, then you must fumigate. This is done by putting the collections into a small room (or large wooden box) and closing all the doors and windows (or the cover). Then put a liquid poison like carbon bisulfide in a couple of dishes high on the shelves in the room and leave for at least two days. The poisonous vapors kill all the pests. Be sure to air out the room (or box) thoroughly afterwards.

BOOKS ON COLLECTING

Many of the books listed at the end of this book in Appendix B give more details on collecting animals and plants than it is possible to give here.

4

Classifying Specimens

HOW TO USE BOOKS

Getting the proper name for a rock, mineral, fossil, animal or plant is one of the most difficult jobs for the museum maker. Some things are fairly easy to name, for example, the birds, about which there are many fine books with lots of color pictures. Others are extremely difficult, as are most insects and many minerals and plants.

From your local library you can get books that will help you name your specimens. Some of these books are listed at the end of this book in Appendix B. Remember that new discoveries in science often make books out of date. Use the latest books you can find on any subject.

Scientific Classification

You are looking for two kinds of names for each specimen you have. One is the common name and the other the scientific name. You ask, why bother with the scientific name? The scientific name is important because very often there are several common names for the same thing or the same name for two different things. For example, the western fence lizard is also called the western swift and the blue-bellied lizard. But it has only one scientific name, *Sceloporus occidentalis*. Again, some people call the cancer crab the rock crab, whereas other people call the shore crabs (*Pachygrapsus* and *Hemigrapsus*) rock crabs. The only way to be sure what is meant is to call each specimen by its scientific name, too.

In using books you need to know the scientific system of classification used by botanists, zoologists, paleontologists and geologists. With geologists it is fairly simple, as usually only one name exists for each kind of rock and mineral. *Quartz,* for example, is both the common and scientific name of this mineral. But the other three sciences use not only common names but also two and sometimes three scientific names for each kind of animal or plant. This is called binomial and trinomial nomenclature.

For use in your museum the binomial (or two-name) system of naming will probably be all you need. Thus animals and plants each have a specific and a generic name. In the case mentioned above of the western fence lizard, *Sceloporus* is the generic name and *occidentalis* is the specific name. For your museum labeling (see next chapter) it is best to underline each scientific name. Put common names in plain or capital letters.

Scientists try to arrange all things in nature into similar groups and these groups into larger groups. This is known as classification. The smallest of these groups is the subspecies, of which there is no need to speak here, since only expert scientists make much use of subspecies. The next smallest group is the species, and then comes the genus. So the wildcat belongs to the species *rufus* and the genus *Lynx*. It is thus called by scientists *Lynx rufus* (Schreber). Schreber is the name of the first scientist who used the name *rufus* to describe the bobcat. Therefore his name is placed after the specific name of the animal to show where that name came from. Knowing the author of a plant or animal name is often important, especially when scientists change a species to a new genus.

The genus *Lynx,* which includes both the wildcat and the Canada lynx as species, is grouped with other catlike creatures into the family Felidae or cats. This family joins with other families, such as the Canidae or dogs and the Ursidae or bears, into the order Carnivora or flesh eaters. The order Carnivora is included with eighteen other orders in the class Mammalia, or animals that give milk to their young. Seven classes of animals then make up the subphylum Vertebrata, or animals with backbones. Four subphyla then make up the largest group of all, the phylum Chordata.

The complete classification of the wildcat can be shown as outlined below:

Phylum Chordata (animals with a nervous chord in the back)
 Subphylum Vertebrata (animals with backbones)
  Class Mammalia (animals that give milk)
   Order Carnivora (meat-eating mammals)
    Family Felidae (cats)
     Genus *Lynx*
      Species *rufus*

Other groups sometimes used are *suborder, superfamily, subfamily, tribe, subgenus* and *subspecies.*
Scientists are not always sure exactly what they mean by spe-

cies. But usually a species may be thought of as Dr. Robert Hegner described it in part: "A group of similar inbreeding animals or plants, capable of producing fertile offspring, and differing from one another only in age, seasonal, sexual or individual characteristics."

Classifying Specimens from Books

Most natural history books give details on how to classify specimens. Many of them have keys to help trace down a specimen to its correct name. Some keys are fairly easy, but most are hard for the beginner. However, the more practice you have with these books and keys the easier the job becomes. Soon you find that the work of classifying an animal or plant is like putting together an exciting puzzle.

Almost all keys make you choose different paths to follow through the key. Rock or mineral keys usually give you many routes to choose from. In the key of *Introduction to the Study of Minerals,* by Dr. Austin F. Rogers, for example, you start off with four choices:

  A. The mineral appears in distinct euhedral crystals.
  B. The mineral has well-defined structure.
  C. The mineral has good to perfect cleavage (or parting).
  D. The mineral is massive without prominent cleavage or any particular structure.

To the beginner this key almost immediately appears too hard to use and you may give up before even trying it. The secret of any key, of course, is to understand what the author means by his or her words. If you are not really interested in minerals, this will seem too hard a job for you. But if you are really interested, you will study the book carefully until you thoroughly understand what is meant by such words as "euhedral" or "cleavage." When you understand the words used in the key, then it soon begins to make sense to you and is a useful tool. You find that classifying minerals with the key is lots of fun.

Most keys are unfortunately not illustrated. Therefore, if you find an illustrated key, you are in luck. I have before me *An Illustrated Key to the Lizards, Snakes and Turtles of the West,* by Jay M. Savage. This key, except for the addition of numerous illustrations, is typical of the keys used for classifying plants and animals. In such a key you start off with two choices, each of which leads to two other choices. This key begins:

1a. Shell absent 14
1b. Shell present 2

If your specimen has a shell (a turtle or a tortoise), you follow down the key until you come to 2. Here again you have:

2a. A hard, inflexible shell present 3
2b. A soft, flexible shell present 13
    Family Trionychidae. SOFT-SHELLED TURTLES

Again you make a choice—say, choosing 2b—and go on then to 13a and 13b, which give you your final choices between:

13a. Anterior (front) border of carapace (shell) with prominent pointed tubercles.
    SPINY SOFT-SHELLED TURTLE. *Amyda spinifera.*
13b. Anterior border of carapace smooth or with slightly developed tubercles.
    EMORY'S SOFT-SHELLED TURTLE. *Amyda emoryi.*

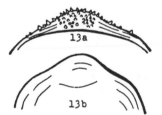

If the front border of the shell is smooth, then the specimen you have in your hand is Emory's soft-shelled turtle.

The greatest trouble with using keys or trying in any other way to learn the name of an animal, plant or rock from a book is lack of patience. You have to be patient and thorough. If you try to hurry too much, you are almost sure to make a mistake. Here are some pointers to help you in this work:

- Always have a good magnifying glass handy (if possible magnifying 10 diameters or more). It will help you look at things too small to see well with just your eyes alone. (Of course, a good binocular microscope of low power is even better.)
- Make sure you know exactly what an author means by each word you find in the book or key. Usually the book will have a glossary that gives the words and explains what they mean. If

not, then you must look them up in a good dictionary. Don't be lazy about this. It is necessary for you to understand. Otherwise mistakes will be very easy to make.

- Even after you have keyed down an animal or plant to what you think is its proper name, find a more complete description in the book if you can and study that. Make sure the appearance of your specimen agrees with the main points in the description.
- Know the geographical locality where your specimen came from and check that against the geographical ranges of species in the book. Many books (including the above reptile key) have maps showing where each species is found. Naturally if your specimen came from Texas, whereas a species you read about lives in Canada, then you don't have the right species even though it may sound right otherwise.
- If you own a book yourself and use it often for learning the names of animals or plants near where you live, then you can save a lot of time by marking it with a colored pencil. Mark each species found near where you live with a colored mark. Then, in using the book, you will be able to quickly find the description of the animal or plant you are holding in your hand.
- For plants, a single-edge razor comes in handy as well as a pair of forceps. With the razor you slice a flower to show the inner arrangement of parts (useful in classifying). With the forceps you pick up small parts and look at them under the magnifying glass.
- Seashore animals, amphibians and other soft-bodied creatures should be studied and classified while they are kept moist in shallow pans of water.
- In classifying plants, they are much easier to work with if they are fresh instead of dry and old. However, you can freshen up even pressed plants by putting the flowers in water. Boiling a pressed flower slightly will also open up its parts.
- Insects that have become hard and stiff are relaxed by placing them in a closed tight tin or jar on top of a blotter placed over wet sand. Leave for two or three days. A few drops of carbolic acid added to the sand will keep the specimens from molding, which they will if there is dampness in the box.
- Remember that illustrations in books may be wrong due to faulty color printing. Carefully study descriptions as well whenever possible.

- As soon as a specimen is named, put the name on a label to keep with it. If you put this off, you are liable to forget. (Labeling is fully described in the next chapter.)
- Whenever possible try to have your specimen's name checked by an expert.

If you wish to have some practice with some very simple and easy keys before you try the more difficult ones, you can find such simple keys to animals, plants, rocks and minerals in a book like my *Amateur Naturalist's Handbook.* Another good source of keys is the *Picture Key Nature Series* published by William C. Brown (see Appendix B for specific titles). Practice with these keys will gradually make you expert in identifying plants, animals and rocks.

HOW TO USE THE HELP OF EXPERTS
AND MUSEUMS

Every beginning collector of plants, animals, rocks and minerals finds out sooner or later that his naming of specimens is not always as easy as it looks. An insect, for example, may look exactly like a picture in a book, but it may be of an entirely different species. Some descriptions of things in books are good, but others are poor or too brief to be very helpful. So the collector who wishes to have a scientifically correct collection needs to have the help of scientists who are experts and specialists.

How easy it is to make a mistake was fully shown to me when I was taking courses in entomology at the University of California. I was learning to identify or name insects by scientific keys and finding the going rough. Many days I would spend more than an hour trying to key down a beetle or other insect to its exact name. I would bring the little creature triumphantly in to my professor, Dr. Van Dyke. I would tell him it was *Dendroctonus monticolae* (Hopkins), the mountain pine beetle, or some similar name, only to be told that I was way off! Painfully I learned that only long practice in this kind of work makes perfect.

An expert can often merely glance at a specimen and tell you instantly what it is. This naturally saves a lot of time, and also helps you learn the names faster. But it does have one drawback, and that is that it takes up the time of the expert to look over your collection and name the specimens for you. Most scientists are very busy and cannot take such time.

In taking or sending specimens to a museum or a specialist for identification there is only one way to get results and at the same time leave a good feeling. That way is to take or send duplicate specimens of the plant or animal you want identified. Offer these in trade for the help you receive. This is the courteous thing to do.

Before sending your specimens to the specialist you should name them yourself at least down to order and preferably down to family. How to do this has already been explained in the first part of this chapter. You must then find the right specialist to send your material to, one who is working particularly in that order or family. (See Chapter 10 for information on where to find lists of museums and scientific specialists.) Such a person will often be glad to name specimens in his or her specialty for you provided you send duplicates that can be kept. Be sure such duplicates are of the same species as that of the specimen you wish identified, and not something that just looks similar. Usually when you are collecting you will put a group of the same species collected into one envelope, jar or bag marked with the same date and location. This will help you to be sure you are sending duplicates of the same species.

Now write to the scientist whose help you want and ask permission to send him or her specimens for identification plus the duplicates. Wait for an answer before sending anything.

The following rules for sending specimens through the mails to a specialist should be observed:

- Label each specimen neatly with order or family name, date, location and any notes you may have about food habits, habitat where found, etc.
- Put all animals or plants of one species close together in the same container and separate from other species. At least four of a kind should be sent if possible and preferably both sexes (if animals).
- Every specimen of insect must be mounted correctly on pins with the labels attached as explained in Chapter 5. To pack for mailing, the greatest possible care must be taken. For insects, glue cork, Masonite or other easily penetrated material to the bottoms of small, strongly made wooden boxes or other containers. Cigar boxes will not do unless strongly reinforced. Pin your specimens tightly in the cork, and if they are large insects use extra pins on both sides of their bodies to hold them tightly in place. Wrap the wooden boxes in corrugated cardboard to prevent shock and also wrap in paper taped on

firmly. Mark your packages FRAGILE and HANDLE WITH CARE.

- Send pressed plants in sheets of newspaper tied and wrapped between two boards. Other specimens also need careful handling. Jars must be wrapped in many layers of paper and shipped in strong boxes.
- Insure your packages, as this is about the only way to make sure the post office will handle them carefully.
- Write a letter to the specialist in which you offer thanks for his or her courtesy, offer duplicates of the species sent, and enclose full postage for the return of your named specimens.

Be careful not to expect or ask too much of these men and women whose expert knowledge you need. Remember that it may take some time, if they are very busy, before they can do the job for you. Be patient and be courteous.

You may also take your specimens to nearby museums and try to identify them by comparing them with similar specimens in the museum. This is not so easy as it sounds, as you may often make mistakes unless you are extremely careful. Things often look alike that are not alike. This is especially true of rocks and minerals. On the other hand, your specimen may sometimes look very different from the museum specimen and yet be of the same species. Starfish of the genus *Linkia,* for example, have different numbers of arms in the same species.

If the museum has what is called a "series" of specimens of the same species, this will help you. You can compare your specimen with the many shown in the series and will probably find some exactly like it if it is the same species. You usually need to get special permission from the museum curator to see these series collections.

Be careful and be patient. Particularly note the geographical locations where the specimens came from. If these locations are a long way from your neighborhood, you probably are looking at the wrong thing. Sometimes, after you think you have identified a specimen, you can take it to the museum curator and ask if you are right. But be careful not to bother such people if they are too busy. If there is any doubt about the name of your specimen, put a question mark (?) on the label where you name it. You can always make a change later.

5

Mounting and Labeling Specimens

The specimens you have obtained have now been classified at least down to family. So you are ready to mount them to show in your museum displays. This preparation for mounting should be made as soon as possible after you collect the specimens and while they are still fresh. However, some things, insects for example, can be stored for a long time without mounting. Plants, once they have gone through the plant press, as described in Chapter 3, can be kept loose in papers for many years before you need to mount them. On the whole, however, it is better to mount your specimens as soon as possible.

MOUNTING AND LABELING
ROCKS AND MINERALS

Rocks and minerals are usually mounted on display boards or in trays or drawers. The trays or drawers are usually divided into square sections and one kind of rock put into each section. A little square or strip of white is painted (with poster paint) on the smoothest part of each rock or mineral. On this you print with black india ink either a number or the name of the rock or mineral plus a number. The number is given again on a sheet of paper pasted or pinned up near the tray. On this sheet opposite each number is the name of the rock or mineral plus any information you have on where it was found and what it is good for.

To put rocks or minerals on a board for a museum display you can use household cement or DuPont's Clear Windshield Sealer. Use plenty of the cement to glue the rock onto the board. If the specimen is too big and heavy for cementing to the board, then you must wire it on. Get a fine small wire, such as picture-hanging wire, from your hardware store. Drill small holes through your plywood or Basalite display board to either side of where you want the specimen to be. Take a hammer and break a couple of pieces from your rock so as to form a groove where the wire can go. Now wire the rock onto the board by running the wire through the groove and through the two holes. Twist the wire tightly together at the back of the board.

On such a display mount you can place a small white paper label directly below each specimen and print the number and name there. Or, it is sometimes possible to letter directly on the board. The trouble with plywood is that ink or paint often run on it. Basalite boards work better, using a yellow or white paint. Make your letters large enough to be seen clearly and letter neatly (see Chapter 9 for information on how to letter).

MOUNTING AND LABELING SOILS AND CHEMICALS

As already explained in Chapter 3, soils and chemicals are usually put into small vials or bottles. A paper label with the name or just a number can be put on each of these bottles. The number is then given on a nearby sheet of paper with the name and a description of the location and uses of each soil or chemical. If these bottles are to be mounted on a display board, they must be carefully wired on as explained above for rocks and minerals.

MOUNTING AND LABELING PLANTS

The method of pressing plants has already been described (see Chapter 3). A plant is usually thoroughly dry and pressed after five or six days in the plant press, especially if the papers or blotters are faithfully changed daily. It is then ready to be mounted on a large sheet of paper as is shown in Figure 7. The sheets from a large scrapbook usually serve very well for this purpose. The plant is fastened to the paper with strips of sticky tape. Or it may be glued with household cement. Cellophane tape of the ordinary kind is not good for the job of taping as it soon dries up and falls off. Get a tape that will hold the plants to the paper for many years. The name, date, location and other interesting facts are put on the label in the lower right-hand corner of the sheet. Do not crowd too many plants onto one sheet.

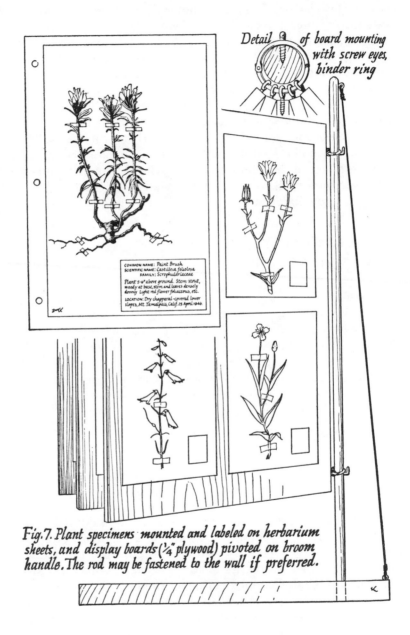

Detail of board mounting with screw eyes, binder ring

COMMON NAME: Paint Brush
SCIENTIFIC NAME: Castilleia foliolosa
FAMILY: Scrophulariaceae

Plant 9-6" above ground. Stem stout,
woody at base, stem and leaves densely
downy. Light red flower foliaceous, etc.

LOCATION: Dry chapparal-covered lower
slopes, Mt. Tamalpais, Calif. 25 April 1946.

Fig. 7. Plant specimens mounted and labeled on herbarium sheets, and display boards (¼" plywood) pivoted on broom handle. The rod may be fastened to the wall if preferred.

These mounted sheets may be displayed in any way you wish, either tacked up on plywood boards to illustrate special museum stories, or kept in books such as scrapbooks. If you wish your specimens preserved for the longest possible time, they should be kept sealed in transparent plastic covers. This is too expensive for most people, however, and is not a necessity.

Very beautiful mounts can be made of seaweed. The method is somewhat different from that used with other plants. The following steps are taken:

1. Float the seaweed specimen on a sheet of strong rag paper in seawater. Use a large flat pan for the water.
2. Lay a strip of cheesecloth over the seaweed.
3. Lift the three parts out of the water together and place inside a folded newspaper sheet.
4. Place this either between heavy blotters or between at least twelve sheets of newspaper on each side.
5. Place in a plant press and buckle tightly or put heavy weights on top of pile.
6. Change blotters or newspapers once a day for at least three days.
7. Remove mount and peel off the cheesecloth from the plant. The seaweed is now stuck to the paper as if it were glued and makes a beautiful mount.
8. Leave the mounted seaweed in an open room for a few days.
9. Mount on a board, in a scrapbook, under transparent plastic, or as desired. Be sure to have a label with each specimen giving name, date collected, where collected and any other interesting information.

One interesting way to mount plants is in an enormous book of plywood or Basalite board pages. A number of 3 × 4 foot plywood boards are attached to a pole by wire rings (see Figure 7). You can mount specimens on each side of each board and arrange them so as to tell an interesting story with pictures and diagrams placed with them. This way of mounting allows a great number of specimens to be shown in a small space.

NOTE: Such a giant book could be used for mounting other types of specimens as well as plants. Rubber models of fossils, tracks and so on would work very well, as they are light and easily glued to the plywood or Basalite pages.

MOUNTING AND LABELING FOSSILS

Fossils, of course, are usually part of a rock. This allows them to be mounted and labeled in much the same way as are rock specimens (see page 44). Often, plaster or rubber casts of fossils can be made, especially when they are difficult to get out of the rock (see Chapter 7 for information on making casts or models). Rubber casts are particularly useful in museum displays since the rubber is light and can easily be cemented onto a display board.

MOUNTING AND LABELING
SEASHORE LIFE

As stated earlier, in Chapter 3, collecting seashore creatures is often forbidden by law. Even if you find a beach where such laws do not apply, you should either not collect out of respect for animal life—and do all your "collecting" by photographing, modeling, drawing or painting specimens—or be absolutely sure you collect only creatures and plants that are obviously in plentiful supply on the beach. Then you can follow the directions given here.

Most animals of the seashore have soft bodies that need to be preserved in a solution of either formalin or alcohol. The formalin is usually put into a 10 percent solution, or one part of formalin to ten parts of water. You can also use 65 to 75 percent undenatured alcohol, or the formula described on page 30. Specimens are kept in jars of different sizes with the labels on the outsides of the jars. Print the name of each animal, the place collected, the date and any other useful information on the labels. Don't crowd your jars with specimens. It is better to have one species in each jar.

Starfish, chitons and crabs can be dried in the sun if the days are hot. They should be spread out on boards. The chitons need to be wired or tied flat on the boards very soon after they are caught (see Figure 8a). Otherwise they curl up into balls. Such specimens can later be mounted on boards with household cement and the names and other important information printed under each specimen. As they fade in color, they can be painted in a lifelike way with oil paints or enamels. Sprayed with transparent plastic they will keep for a long time.

A beautiful way to mount seashore life to display colors and shapes to the best advantage is shown in Figure 8b. Two sheets of

Fig.8.(a) *Wiring chiton to a board to dry flat.*

(b) *Making a display mount of seashore life. Seal glass on one side with putty and lay frame down to place specimen and supports, and fill with preservative. Then put other glass side in place and seal it up.*

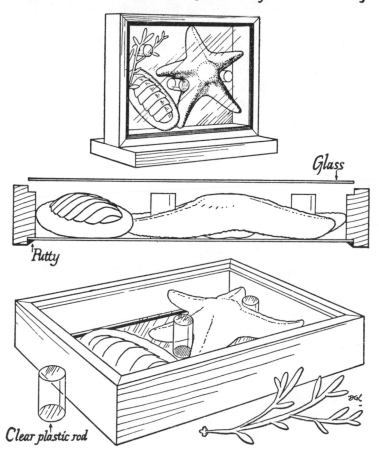

Glass

Putty

Clear plastic rod

glass are sealed with DuPont's Clear Windshield Sealer into a waterproofed board frame that has been well varnished. The sheets of
glass are put close enough together so that both sides of each animal
to be mounted will be against or very near the glass. After the specimens have been placed inside they must be blocked in place by small
blocks of transparent plastic cut to fit exactly between the two glass
sheets. These plastic blocks are cemented in place while the mount
is lying flat on a table. When all specimens are in place and cemented
there if necessary, the mount is placed upright in a holding stand.
The space between the glass walls is filled with clear preservative
(either 10 percent formalin solution or 75 percent alcohol). The top
is then sealed on with waterproof sealing cement and the whole
mount made so it can be turned in any direction without leaking.

This mount may be hung on a wall, but the best place for it is on
a holding stand (as shown) in the middle of a table. Light can then be
directed through the glass from either side and all the beautiful
colors shown. This is a particularly good way to mount and display
such delicate and beautiful specimens as hydroids or nudibranches.
Labels may be placed around the sides of this mount telling the story
of the animals displayed. Keep displays out of direct sunlight!

MOUNTING AND LABELING INSECTS
AND SIMILAR CREATURES

NOTE: Insects are usually so plentiful that it is possible to collect
them without doing any harm, as noted in Chapter 3, but always be
careful not to collect and mount the following kinds of insects: 1)
those that are very rare—ask at your nearest college or university
entomology department about this; 2) those that are good allies of
mankind in fighting insect pests—unless you find such insects in
large numbers; or 3) insects or related creatures that are very poisonous, such as the black widow spider. Only experts should handle
these poisonous creatures. Ask about these insects at your nearest
college or museum entomology department.

Worms, spiders and soft-bodied insect larvae require different
treatment than do the hard-bodied insects. They must usually be
put into small glass bottles or vials with alcohol. The alcohol
strength should be gradually increased for spiders from about 70 to
90 percent or more. This should be done over a period of several
weeks with a change of 5 percent made about once a week. Another
solution in which these soft-bodied creatures may be kept is de-

scribed on page 30. The best place to obtain alcohol for scientific purposes is through a college or university. Explain your needs to a professor in the biology department, and he or she should be able to help you. Each vial or bottle containing specimens has a label on the outside on which is typed or hand-printed with india ink the name, location collected, the date and any other important information.

Caterpillars may be inflated with hot air and preserved in the way shown in Figure 9. You lay the freshly killed caterpillar on a piece of glass and roll a round pencil over it from the head to the tail. This is repeated until most of the insides have been forced out the tail end. A glass tube with a small opening in a pointed end is forced into the caterpillar's tail opening. Hot air is forced through the tube by bellows as shown in the figure until the caterpillar is puffed up with air to its usual life size. A wire is attached to the end of the caterpillar (as shown) and then the specimen is mounted on a pin.

Figure 10 shows the mounting of hard-bodied insects on cotton under glass in what is called a Riker mount. Butterflies, moths and dragonflies are mounted on their backs against a soft board or piece of Celotex or cork. The wings are spread at right angles to the body and pinned down in place with strips of paper. At the end of about

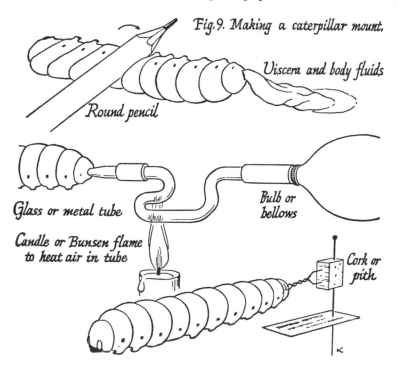

Fig. 9. Making a caterpillar mount.

Viscera and body fluids

Round pencil

Glass or metal tube

Bulb or bellows

Candle or Bunsen flame to heat air in tube

Cork or pith

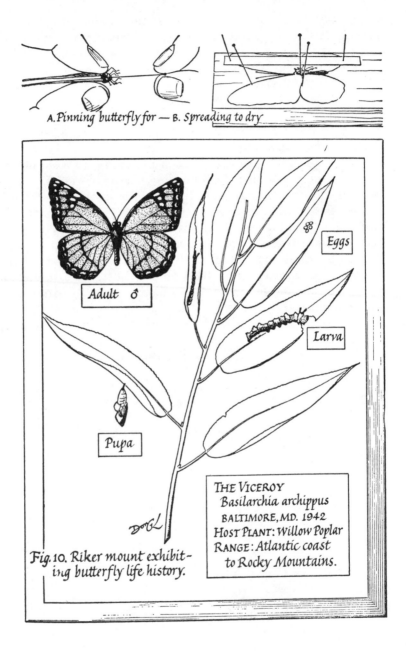

A. *Pinning butterfly for* — B. *Spreading to dry*

Eggs

Adult ♂

Larva

Pupa

THE VICEROY
  Basilarchia archippus
  BALTIMORE, MD. 1942
  HOST PLANT: *Willow Poplar*
  RANGE: *Atlantic coast
    to Rocky Mountains.*

*Fig. 10. Riker mount exhibit-
ing butterfly life history.*

five days they are ready to be mounted on the cotton. Other insects are mounted directly on the cotton when freshly killed. With a pair of forceps or a pin, tease the legs out into natural positions. When pressed down on the cotton by the glass the insects soon dry and hold their positions. Labels should be printed with name, date and location captured, and placed under the glass below each insect (as shown in Figure 10).

Flat-box mounts of the type shown in the figure are easily made. Take a handkerchief or similar flat cardboard box and cut out the center of the top, leaving a rim about ½ inch wide. Then into the top glue a sheet of glass that fits it perfectly. The lower half of the box should be filled with dry-goods cotton to the top of the sides. Over this place a smooth layer of drugstore cotton and upon it the bodies of the insects. The back of such mounts must be sprinkled with mothball crystals or paradichloride of benzene crystals to guard against pests. When the mount is completed pin the cover of the box to the lower part with long pins stuck through the sides into the cotton. The sides can be sealed with strong plastic tape.

Insects become dry and hard within a few days after they have been killed. It is thus far better to mount them when they are freshly killed. But if you wish to relax them for mounting after they have become dry, it is quite easy. Take a jar or tightly covered tin box and fill the lower half with wet sand. Put a couple of blotters over this and put your insects on the blotters. A few drops of carbolic acid added to the sand will prevent mold. At the end of two or three days you will find the insects completely relaxed and ready to be mounted.

Figure 11 shows ways of mounting insects on pins. (Insect pins can be obtained from the places mentioned in Appendix C at the end of this book.) Note the places in the insects' bodies through which the pins are pushed. Use the right place for the right insect. The back of the insect should be about ⅜ inch from the top of the pin.

Spreading boards (such as those pictured) are easily made out of soft wood with Celotex or cork along the bottom of the groove as shown in the figure. It is better to have the boards slant inward to the groove as shown, but flat boards will also do. Pin the wings of butterflies, moths, dragonflies, grasshoppers and so on in place with strips of paper. Remove the strips at the end of about five days when the insects are dry and ready for mounting. Wings should be at right angles to the body as shown. Other insects, such as beetles, plant bugs and wasps, are better mounted on cardboard or bristol board stretched between two boards nailed to a Celotex base, as is also shown in Figure 11 The boards are ¾ inch thick, which will place the

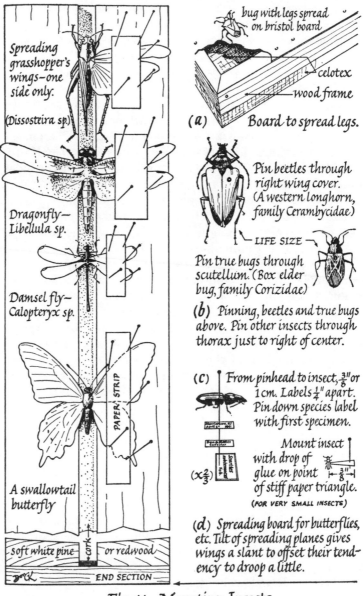

Spreading grasshopper's wings—one side only.

(Dissosteira sp.)

Dragonfly— Libellula sp.

Damsel fly— Calopteryx sp.

PAPER STRIP

A swallowtail butterfly

soft white pine cork or redwood

END SECTION

bug with legs spread on bristol board

celotex

wood frame

(a) Board to spread legs.

Pin beetles through right wing cover. (A western longhorn, family Cerambycidae)

— LIFE SIZE —

Pin true bugs through scutellum. (Box elder bug, family Corizidae)

(b) Pinning, beetles and true bugs above. Pin other insects through thorax just to right of center.

(c) From pinhead to insect, $\frac{3}{8}$" or 1 cm. Labels $\frac{1}{4}$" apart. Pin down species label with first specimen.

($\times\frac{2}{3}$)

Mount insect with drop of glue on point of stiff paper triangle.

$\frac{3}{8}$"

(FOR VERY SMALL INSECTS)

(d) Spreading board for butterflies, etc. Tilt of spreading planes gives wings a slant to offset their tendency to droop a little.

Fig. 11. Mounting Insects.

insect about right on the pin when the pin is shoved through the cardboard and down to the Celotex base. Spread the legs of the insect in a natural way on the cardboard surface with a pin. Change cardboards when the first one gets too many pinholes in it.

White filing cards can be cut up to make insect labels. Use india ink and print on the label with a small pen such as a crow quill. Make your lettering small and neat (see Figure 11). Put the labels near the insects you are mounting and later put them on the pin, as shown, when the insect is mounted in a box. The first label, about ½ inch up on the pin, should give the place and date collected. The second label, about ¼ inch up on the pin, should give the name of the collector. The third label, stuck by the pin against the bottom of the display box, should have on it the common and scientific names of the insect. The appearance of these labels is shown in Figure 11.

Figure 12 shows the kinds of boxes used for mounting specimens. While cigar boxes can be used, they are not too satisfactory because insect pests can easily get into them and eat your specimens. In all boxes it is necessary to sprinkle mothball flakes or paradichloride of benzene crystals to discourage such pests. Do this at least every three months.

For museum displays it is best to have your specimens mounted in boxes with glass covers. Such boxes can themselves be mounted on plyboard and put on the wall of your room. The glass must be fitted into a hinged cover as shown in Figure 12. Keep covers tightly closed at all times. Such boxes can be bought from the companies listed in Appendix C. Books on woodworking listed in Appendix B will help you make them.

Insects can be mounted for display purposes on a flat board or as part of a natural-looking mounted display in a glass case as shown in Figure 12. The legs are glued in natural positions with household cement. But all such mounted insects must be sprayed with liquid transparent plastic (spray cans can be bought at most hardware stores). This preserves them from pests. If dust gathers on these specimens, it must be carefully brushed off with a wet paintbrush.

MOUNTING AND LABELING REPTILES AND AMPHIBIANS

NOTE: As suggested in Chapter 3, I urge you to do most if not all of your collecting of amphibians and reptiles with a camera, modeling material, drawing or painting. However, if you find that you can col-

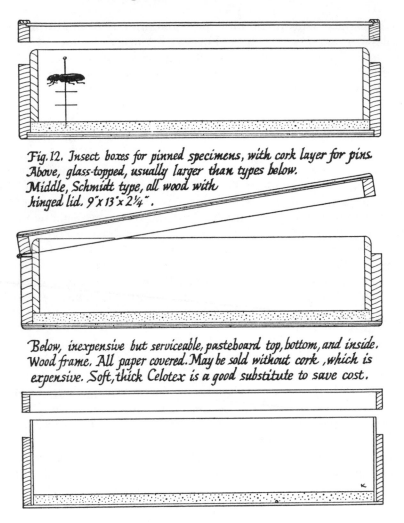

Fig. 12. Insect boxes for pinned specimens, with cork layer for pins. Above, glass-topped, usually larger than types below. Middle, Schmidt type, all wood with hinged lid. 9″x 13″x 2¼″.

Below, inexpensive but serviceable, pasteboard top, bottom, and inside. Wood frame. All paper covered. May be sold without cork, which is expensive. Soft, thick Celotex is a good substitute to save cost.

lect some species without breaking any law, then use the following information for mounting specimens.

Most reptiles and amphibians (frogs, toads and salamanders) are preserved in jars full of either formalin solution or undenatured alcohol. Of the two, alcohol is the better as it keeps the specimens relaxed, but it is also harder to get and is more expensive.

For frogs, toads, salamanders and smooth-skinned lizards use a 6 percent formalin solution. This means one part of formalin (purchased from a drugstore) to sixteen parts of water. For most reptiles use a 10 percent formalin solution, or one part of formalin to ten parts of water. Even if you plan to use alcohol, both reptiles and amphibians should be placed in the formalin solution first for at least twenty-four hours.

To put your specimens in alcohol, first take them out of the formalin solution and wash thoroughly, allowing water to pour over them for several minutes. Then place most reptiles in 75 percent alcohol. Place amphibians and smooth-skinned lizards in 65 percent alcohol.

All specimens should have tiny slits cut at regular intervals down the middle of their bellies and throats with a single-edge razor or a sharp knife. This allows the formalin or alcohol to enter inside the bodies and help preserve them.

Each specimen should have a label attached to the foot or body by a string. On this label mark with black india ink the number, name (if identified), the date, the place captured and any other important information. Use the same number in your notes about the specimen. Each jar containing specimens should be labeled on the outside with the same sort of information.

Snakes and lizards may be skinned with a single-edge razor or sharp knife. These skins are good for display mounts of different types of reptile skins, but the job of mounting such skins on a clay or wax body cannot be done very satisfactorily save by an expert. One reason is that the skins usually stretch too much in skinning, so that the mounted animal does not have its natural appearance. It is far better to make a rubber, wax or plaster model as described in Chapter 7.

To skin a snake or lizard, cut down the middle of the belly. Be careful not to cut through into the intestines. Work the skin free from the flesh with your fingers. On lizards, make side cuttings down the middle of the undersides of the legs. A snake is soon stripped of its skin, except for the skin of the head, which is often hard to get off. If too hard, cut off the head. For completing the skinning of lizards, follow the directions given for mammals on pages 60–62 up to Number 14. Skins of lizards or snakes should be pinned out on a flat board (bottom side up) and rubbed with salt and alum and allowed to dry in the sun. Keep a correctly filled-out label with each skin.

After these skins are dry they may be unpinned and turned around facedown on your final mounting board. Here they are pinned or glued and any information about them printed below each skin.

It is possible to get complete skeletons of snakes or lizards by putting the dead animal on an anthill or nest. Small carnivorous ants are best, as they will strip away all the flesh from the skeletons in a few days. The skeletons must then be carefully cleaned in warm water and bleach, and all dirt and skin removed. Glue any broken parts of the skeletons back into place and mount the skeletons on a flat board with household cement to hold them on. Label each specimen with name, date collected, location and any other interesting information.

MOUNTING AND LABELING MAMMALS

NOTE: Mammals which are very numerous or are pests to human crops may be collected and killed for specimens, as explained in Chapter 3, then mounted as explained in this chapter, but rare species and those useful to humans should not be captured or killed and then mounted. Use photographs, modeling, paintings, etc., instead. Ask your local fish and wildlife agency about this.

The fur, bones, teeth, etc., of mammals may be glued or wired with small wires to a display board. Under each specimen, print a label giving the name and where and when collected, as:

> CANINE TOOTH OF WILDCAT
> WILDCAT CANYON, BERKELEY, CALIFORNIA
> JUNE 25, 1984

For a special display on teeth you may want to add information about how that particular kind of tooth is used. In some displays where there is no room and your main idea is to tell a story, it is not necessary to put the date and place, but only the name and any information that is important in your story.

The mounting of mammals in museum displays, known as the art of taxidermy, takes careful study and training. The books on taxidermy listed at the end of this book in Appendix B will give you the full details you need. Watching or getting help from an expert taxidermist can also aid greatly in this difficult work.

In this book there is only room to tell you how to make a study skin of a mammal. A study skin is a stuffed skin such as is used by scientists in their mammal collections. It is not very good for making a museum display as the animal is not mounted in a lifelike manner.

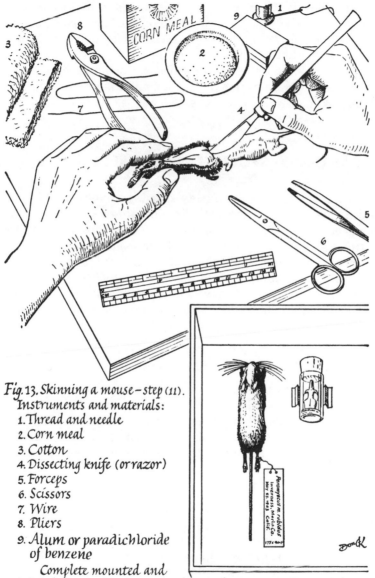

Fig. 13. Skinning a mouse — step (11).
Instruments and materials:
1. Thread and needle
2. Corn meal
3. Cotton
4. Dissecting knife (or razor)
5. Forceps
6. Scissors
7. Wire
8. Pliers
9. Alum or paradichloride of benzene
   Complete mounted and
labeled mouse skin in storage box or drawer. Skull in a vial.

However, making study skins is good practice before you go on to the more difficult job of mounting mammals in lifelike poses. You can also use study skins in some kinds of museum displays, particularly when you are trying to show variations in color, shape and size of mammals within one genus or species.

Figure 13 shows the tools needed for skinning and also illustrates some of the steps in skinning a small mammal. Larger mammals are skinned in much the same way as here described for a mouse.

SKINNING AND STUFFING A MOUSE

Your mouse should be freshly killed, and you should have the following materials to work with: 1) some thin white or gray thread and a needle, 2) some cornmeal (used for drying up blood), 3) a roll of cotton batting, 4) a very sharp knife or single-edge razor, 5) a pair of forceps, 6) a pair of small, sharp scissors, 7) a foot or so of ¹⁄₁₆ inch wire, 8) a pair of pliers, and 9) alum or crushed paradichloride of benzene crystals. (It is wise to wash your hands thoroughly after you use alum or paradichloride of benzene crystals so that you will not get either in your mouth, though neither is particularly harmful.)

WARNING: Do not handle a dead or sick rodent you find on the ground. It may have a very dangerous disease!

Before you start skinning, measure the mouse from nose tip to tail tip. Measure also the length of the tail, the length of the hind foot and the exact length of the ears. These measurements should all be written or painted neatly with ink on a small card, ½ × 2½ inches. Also on this card should be the name of the kind of mouse and where and when it was captured. For lengths, it is really more scientific to use metric measurements.

> ○ #11 *Peromyscus maniculatus*, Deer Mouse
> April 10, 1984, Coose Bay, Oregon
> Total Length 6¼ in. Tail 2¾ in.
> ○ Hind foot ⅝ in. Ear ½ in.

This card is later tied to the leg of the finished specimen with a short string run through two holes poked in the end of the card. The following are the steps to be taken in skinning a mouse:

1. Place your mouse back down on a wide smooth board and cut through the skin of the stomach and directly in the middle with your small scissors.
2. Carefully cut the skin up the middle of the body until you reach the throat. Be careful not to open up the insides. Wherever blood appears blot it up with the cornmeal, which you should use freely.
3. From the central opening now cut with your scissors down the middle of each hind leg through the skin and about two-thirds of the way up to the first joint.
4. With your sharp knife or razor begin cutting the skin away from the anus (opening by the tail). Work until you can force the skin back with your fingers and your thumb and forefinger meet around the back of the mouse under the skin. At the same time work the skin toward the back all along the sides of the body.
5. When you have the skin free from the fleshy parts of the hind legs and have worked it down to the first joint, take your scissors and cut through the thigh bone on each hind leg about halfway between the joints.
6. You can then cut the meat off the remaining part of each bone with your scissors until there is little left. Leave these cleaned leg bones attached to the skin.
7. Working now mainly with your fingers, push the skin off the back and away from the anus. Use the razor when muscles get in the way until only the tail in the back still has the skin on. You must be very careful not to cut the skin around the tail.
8. The bony tail must now be pulled right out of its skin. This job you should do entirely with your fingers, rubbing them along the bone and pushing carefully. At the same time, with the fingers of the other hand, you pull at the tip of the tail. Often the skin will come right off the tail with little trouble, if you will just be patient.

   Now the whole back part of the skin is free from the body.
9. With the scissors again, cut slits down the middle of each foreleg two-thirds of the way to the joint.
10. Cut the fleshy part of each leg through the middle, halfway between the joints. Then work the skin down the legs with your fingers until you can cut away the meat from the remaining leg bones. You can now push the skin away from

the body with your fingers until the skin is free from all but the head.

11. On the head you work mainly with the sharp razor or knife (see Figure 13). Keep pulling the skin back over the head as you cut, pushing the skin with your fingers. Wherever it seems stuck cut it carefully free.

12. The first things to watch for on the head are the ears. Only experience will tell you when and where to cut these. They will appear first as small gray lumps. These must be cut across with the razor as close to the head as possible.

13. When the ears are free, your next problem is the eyes. These appear as black lumps toward the front of the head. Cut through the film that covers the eyes as far back on the head as you can. Then carefully cut through the eye edges until the skin that is attached to them is free.

14. Last come the nose and the lips. You must cut through the fleshy inner part of the lips, both upper and lower, until at last the skin gives way and comes entirely free from the body.

    You can now make a mounted specimen—or study skin, as the naturalists call it. Throw away the body, but keep the head, as later you are going to have to clean out the skull.

15. Take your needle and thread and sew the two lips together, tying with a single knot at their tips.

16. Take your alum or paradichloride of benzene, and, after most of the flesh has been scraped free, sprinkle and rub the preservative all over the inside of the skin.

17. Cut a piece of the thin wire about an inch longer than the tail. Around this roll a thin sheet of cotton, moistened slightly with water. Do this until the wire and cotton are about as thick as the original fleshy part of the tail.

18. Now carefully shove this down into the empty tail skin. Be sure that the end of the wire does not poke through the skin.

19. You may have to take off some of the cotton if the wire won't go in easily.

20. Similar but shorter wires are wrapped with cotton for the legs and shoved down the legs between the skin and the bone. In each case let ½ to ¾ inch of the wire stick out into the body opening.

21. Then take some of the cotton and roll it into a roll of about the same size as the body of the mouse.

22. Take your forceps and tightly pinch together one end of this

roll. You fold it and work it with your forceps until you get a hard "nose" of cotton.

23. Hold this nose tightly together with the forceps and stick it into the head of the mouse so that "nose" meets nose.
24. Pull the skin up over the cotton so that the cotton is entirely inside.
25. Take your needle and thread and begin to sew the skin together carefully from the throat down to the tail. Take care to pull the two skin edges tightly together.
26. When the skin is all sewed up, take the mouse in your hands and straighten out the legs and tail in a natural manner. Then work the body with your fingers until the shape appears as it did in life. Brush the skin carefully with a small brush until all the hair is lying down and smooth.
27. Now you must tie to one of the specimen's legs the card illustrated on page 60.
28. The skull has been cut free from the body and you must cut away all meat that you find on the outside of the skull.
29. Clean out the skull by means of a brain spoon (made by whittling a tiny wooden spoon). Dip this spoon again and again into the brain cavity until most of the brain matter is gone.
30. Dry this clean skull in the sun and let ants finish the job of cleaning it. Then place the skull in a small glass bottle or cardboard box with a number that is the same as the number on the card you tied to the leg of the mounted specimen. The appearance of the complete mount is shown in Figure 13.

If you do all this carefully, you will have a scientific specimen for your collection. It sounds like a lot of trouble, but expert naturalists have trained themselves to skin and mount a mouse in five minutes!

MOUNTING AND LABELING BIRDS

Remember that the killing of most birds is prohibited or regulated by law on account of their value to mankind in controlling harmful insect and rodent populations. Find out from your local Department of Fish and Game exactly which birds can be killed for specimens. In most cases it is better to use photographs, models, carvings, paintings, etc., for your museum.

Bird bones, feathers, bills and feet can be collected, mounted and labeled as described above for mammal teeth, bones and fur. Skinning and mounting a bird is even more difficult than the job of mounting a mammal.

The job of skinning a bird is done in much the same way as skinning a mouse, but with the following differences.

1. Because of the more delicate nature of bird skins, be sure to take much more care in this skinning (see Figure 14).
2. Cut the leg and wing bones away from the inside of the skin, as is explained with the mouse, but use special care in pushing back the delicate skin from the legs, as the skin may easily be broken.
3. Cut the tailbone through right next to the skin, so that only the last joint remains attached to the skin and tail feathers.
4. When the main part of the skin and the limbs are cut away from the body, work carefully with the knife to cut the skin away from the neck. Don't try to pull the skin away from the skull.
5. Now pull the skin up across the back half of the skull and cut off the lower part of the skull with your sharp knife. This allows the face skin to hold the front part of the skull attached to the bill.
6. Use a small brain spoon to thoroughly clean out the remaining part of the skull still attached to the skin. Small birds can have the eyeballs left in the head, but you must work the eyes out of the skulls of larger birds very carefully and replace them with artificial eyes or marbles.
7. Carefully clean away all flesh from the legs and corners of the skin. Then powder and rub them well with alum or crushed paradichloride of benzene crystals to protect against pests. Put some of this chemical into all parts of the skull.
8. With a small round stick that you have cut so it fits exactly the bird's length from inside the skull to the tail's base, create a central core around which you will form the body. The end placed inside the skull must be wadded in place with cotton.
9. Use wire thick enough to fit the size of the bird (thicker for larger birds), to support the legs and wings. Run a wire

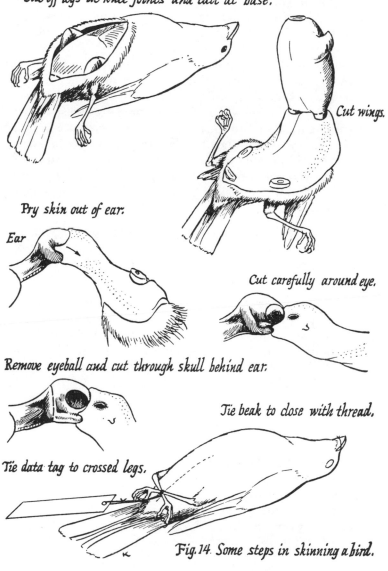

Cut off legs at knee joints and tail at base.

Cut wings.

Pry skin out of ear.

Ear

Cut carefully around eye.

Remove eyeball and cut through skull behind ear.

Tie beak to close with thread.

Tie data tag to crossed legs.

Fig. 14. Some steps in skinning a bird.

down each leg between the bones and the skin until a firm support is given. Attach the other end of the wire to the middle stick.

10. Wrap the whole stick with cotton to give fullness and the proper shape to the body of the bird. Dampen first.

11. Carefully sew the bird together so that it appears natural (see Figure 14); carefully brush the feathers to smooth them. Put the stuffed bird away in a dry place for several days to let the skin harden so that the form is preserved. Tie to the foot a label which gives the name of the specimen, its catalog number and the date it was collected. This information can be used to head entries in your museum notebook, which will provide extensive information on such things as where you obtained the specimen, the specimen's measurements and a detailed description of the habitat where collected.

NOTE: It is against the law to collect birds' eggs unless you have a special permit to do so. However, you may find eggs spilled out of nests onto the ground, and these can be used for a museum as stated above.

Fresh birds' eggs are blown free of yolk and white by cutting two small holes, one at each end of each egg, and blowing hard with the mouth at one hole to force the insides out of the other hole. Each egg should be mounted on cotton in a small box and labeled correctly. Eggs may also be placed in specimens of nests, provided you put the right eggs in the right nests.

CONCLUSION

It is important to use the utmost neatness and care in mounting and labeling your specimens. Follow directions closely and work hard until you have nearly perfect mounts. These will attract the attention and admiration of everyone. Some books that will help you further with this work are listed in the bibliography in Appendix B at the end of this book.

6

Collecting Pictures
and Photographs

Pictures and photographs add a great deal to your museum, especially if they are in color. Black and white photographs and other pictures, too, can of course be colored. A set of transparent oil colors (useful also in coloring wax and rubber models) should be used for coloring photographs. Other pictures can be colored with watercolors. Books that teach you how to color are listed in Appendix B.

Magazines are a wonderful source of pictures. If you can get old magazines nobody wants, so much the better, as you can cut out pictures from them to your heart's content. Make a file of these pictures in a scrapbook, putting all the pictures about mammals in one section, about birds in another, about plants in a third, and so on. These will then be ready whenever you plan a new museum display.

Especially collect large pictures in color. Old calendars have very large and beautiful color pictures, some of which show scenes of nature. *National Geographic* magazine has many fine color pictures, though these are not as large as one might like. *Natural History* magazine is another good magazine for color pictures and others.

Old books are another place where you may find pictures you can cut out and use. Be sure, however, that you cut out nothing that somebody else owns and wants.

To get many photographs of your own you naturally need a camera. This book can only suggest you talk about cameras with someone who is an expert on photography, and buy the best camera you can afford. However, even a small, cheap camera can often take good pictures. Books to help you take good wildlife photographs are listed in Appendix B.

For your museum displays you need enlargements of your photographs, at least 5 × 7 inches and preferably much bigger. Careful coloring of such a photographic enlargement before mounting will greatly add to its beauty and interest. If you can get your own photographic enlarger and enlarge pictures yourself, you will be in a position to get copies of many fine photographs from the negatives of friends in exchange for enlarging their pictures.

Seek photographs and pictures that will best help explain the story you are trying to tell in a museum display. For example, if you are making an exhibit of life on the Great Plains, photos not only of typical Plains scenery but of the animals and plants found there would prove useful.

To protect both pictures and photographs and show them to best advantage in your museum displays, you can frame them and cover them with glass. An inexpensive cardboard frame made from an old cardboard box and with the glass taped on is often all that is necessary.

The right picture or photograph in the right place is important. Pictures should not be so out of place in a display that they take away interest instead of helping it. For example, a brightly colored picture set up in one corner of an otherwise dull-colored museum display will take away interest from the main part of the display. Pictures should harmonize with the display and seem like part of it. There is more discussion of this need in Chapter 9. Plans 2 and 5 show a harmonious arrangement of pictures in museum displays.

Pictures that catch the true beauty of natural scenes are best to use. Hunt for beautiful pictures as you would hunt for valuable stamps if you were a good stamp collector. Sometimes you can trade pictures with other museum makers and so obtain the ones you need for your displays (see Chapter 10). There is no feeling quite so satisfying as seeing a picture or photograph fit perfectly into your museum exhibit, helping to make the whole thing take on new life and meaning.

7

Plaster, Rubber and Wax Molds and Models

Now we take up a subject that is a most fascinating one to any museum maker. It is how to make model figures that help tell your story in a lifelike way. Most of us are not sculptors. Far from it. When we try to mold a figure out of clay or cut it out of soap, we can rarely do a job that looks professional. So this book is not going to try to tell you how to be a soap carver or a clay modeler.

What this chapter gives are instructions on how to make casts or models of things that already exist. It tells you how to make model leaves, for example, or models of snakes and lizards or little figures of humans and animals. By learning how to make casts of these things you can make models that will look as good and professional as anything a real expert could do with clay or soapstone or wood. However, if you have a natural talent for carving or modeling, get a good book or books on the subject and learn how (see Appendix B).

COPYING ANIMAL TRACKS

Let us suppose, for example, that you are working on a set of animal tracks to be done in plaster casts. First you find a place where animals have left tracks, such as on the muddy shore of a stream or pond. You fix with cellophane tape a round rim of cardboard about an inch wide and big enough to surround the track you are going to make a copy of. This you place around the track. Into this form (as shown in Figure 15) you pour a mixture of plaster of paris and water, made like a thick cream. (For more detailed instructions on making a plaster–water mixture, see pages 73 and 75.) This hardens enough within half an hour to take up from the ground.

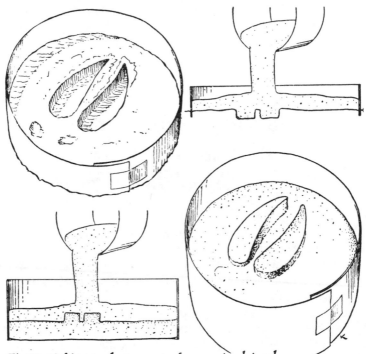

Fig. 15. Making a plaster cast of an animal track.

You have at this stage only the negative or mold of your track. To make the positive, or final, model, you must first thoroughly wash, clean and dry your negative. Dry by putting in a hot place in the sun or in a small open box directly under a forty-watt light bulb for several hours. Following this, paint the upper surface of the plaster negative with a film of white liquid shellac or liquid soap (made by mixing soap chips in hot water). This coating should be allowed to dry and will help prevent the new plaster of paris you are going to pour from sticking to the old.

Again place a circular rim of cardboard around your negative to hold in the cast plaster (or you may use a wall made of modeling or other clay an inch high). You now pour over the negative a smooth, thick, creamy mixture of plaster of paris and water. When this hardens, it can be easily taken away from your negative, and there you have your final copy or model of the animal track.

Each copy of a track made in this way should be painted with a dark paint, probably brown. This makes the track stand out against the white plaster and produces a very pleasing display. Tracks so made can be mounted with wire or household cement on a plyboard or Basalite board to be hung on your wall, or they can be arranged in a display case to tell an interesting story of animal or bird tracks. Rubber models can also be made of such tracks from your plaster molds (see page 81).

MAKING MODELS OF ACTUAL ANIMALS OR PLANTS OR CASTING FROM MADE MODELS

Making stuffed specimens of animals so they will look lifelike is such a difficult job, requiring real skill and long training, that the work is very discouraging to beginners. That is why in this book only brief descriptions of how to make study skins of animals and birds are given (see Chapter 5) and no attempt is made to show how to make lifelike mounts of these creatures through the taxidermy method. It is necessary to study complete books on this difficult subject.

However, the amateur can much more rapidly learn to make plaster-of-paris or rubber molds of natural objects, plants or animals. From these molds, plaster, wax or rubber casts or models can be made, perfect in form, and painted in a lifelike way. This is particularly possible because scientific advances have brought us new, simpler and more easily learned methods of making casts and molds. The great advantage these models of life have is that they keep the color and natural shape almost forever and there is no danger of their decaying or being eaten by insect pests. Appendix C lists addresses of model materials suppliers. Booklets written by these suppliers will tell you what the different materials can be used for and how to use the materials.

Because we should deemphasize the actual collecting of valuable animal and plant life, you should consider making casts of models already made of plants and animals. Sometimes you can find these models in the homes of your friends. Or you might try a museum. When you do the latter, be extremely courteous and explain how you will be using your models for purposes of education and better understanding of the world and its life. If you can't find models to base your own models on, you can buy ready-made models from stores that sell hobby equipment, art objects, etc.; often museum stores sell such models. You can then make casts of these models and make extra models which you can sell to other amateur museum makers or use for trading purposes.

The following instructions on making casts of animal or plant specimens also describe how to make casts of models already in existence.

Plants, reptiles, amphibians, fish, worms and seashore life are more easily put into this model form than mammals or birds. In any case the beginner should try the easier things first.

Three general types of material are best used for making molds (negatives) and casts (positives) of animals and plants. These are 1) plaster of paris, 2) rubber or latex mixtures, and 3) resin–wax mixtures. The resin–wax mixtures are used only for producing the casts or models (positives).

In using any of these materials it is wise to know what would be best for any particular job. For the beginner the models of rubber or plaster are easier to make and handle, but the resin–wax models are sometimes better for delicate work, especially with plants. Examples of displays where model figures can be used effectively are shown in this book in Plans 2, 3 and 5. In the model of the tide pool in Plan 2, for example, rocks are arranged to show the appearance of the tide pool. On these rocks (or artificial rocks made of papier-mâché) are placed models and actual specimens of the animals and plants that are found there, all glued to the rocks in lifelike positions.

Whether to use real specimens or models of these specimens depends entirely on the nature of the animal or plant. Certain plants, particularly the coralline algae of the seashore, can be sprayed or brushed with shellac or transparent plastic and will continue to look lifelike for years. The shells of shellfish and the dried and painted specimens of crabs can also be used. But most animals and plant specimens fade, decay or are subject to insect pests. For them rubber, plaster or wax models are far more permanent and effective. Most museum casting of such models is now being done with latex or rubber compounds in plaster molds.

Plaster-of-Paris Molds

Plaster of paris can be bought in most hardware stores very cheaply. Because of its cheapness and the simplicity of its use, the beginner had better practice with plaster molds before trying other materials. The following are the steps to be taken in making molds of animals and plants with plaster of paris:

1. Be sure your animal has been freshly killed in such a way that it is relaxed. Reptiles and amphibians may be killed by

putting them in a tight tin box or jar in which has been placed cotton saturated with ether. Keep this closed for at least a half-hour. Or you may drown reptiles in *warm* water filled to the top of a tightly covered jar (to keep out air).

2. Get the animal to look alive by the natural way you place it. A cast of a *dead-looking* animal looks even deader.

3. To make it look lifelike place the animal on a clay or cardboard pallet in a cardboard box which has been lined with waxed paper to allow freeing of the plaster mold later. Put corrugated cardboard under the box for aid in holding pins used in anchoring. This anchoring prevents the specimen's floating when denser plaster is poured over it (see Figure 16a). Potters' used clay is cheap to get, or modeling clay can be used.

4. Mucus-secreting animals such as salamanders, fish, toads and frogs should be bathed in strong alum solution to take off the slime. The slime may prevent the plaster from setting properly and give you a bad mold. With all lung-breathing animals you should fill the throat with a wad of wet cotton to stop the pressure of the plaster from forcing out a "burp," which would leave a bubble in your plaster mold.

5. In arranging your animal in the box, don't worry about undercuts (any parts of the mold where the body of an animal curves under the mold surface) so long as the animal can later be pulled out of the mold. However, angled or bent legs should be attached by clay strips underneath to the clay or cardboard pallet for removal (see Figure 16b).

6. When possible, get the head of the animal lifted up in a natural way by sticking a pin through it if necessary. This allows plaster to get on all sides of the head for greater detail (see Figure 16c).

7. Fasten the animal at different places with slender, headless pins thrust at an angle through to the box bottom and into the corrugated cardboard. (Regular household pins can be used if their heads are snipped off, but longer pins are preferable.) If dimples appear around pins, lift the animal *up the pin* and adjust to remove dimple (see Figure 16d). It is best to pin each limb and the tail in two or three places, snakes in several places. Snakes are best mounted on a cardboard rather than a clay pallet.

8. A hard rubber or pottery dish or bowl should be filled with

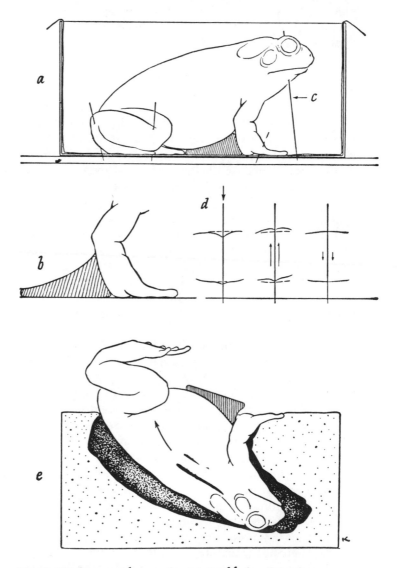

Fig.16. Making a plaster-of-paris mold in one piece.

the correct amount of water (practice will teach you this amount). Have enough plaster and some to spare for your job. To have to mix up another batch of plaster right in the middle of your work is a great annoyance.

9. Some kind of coloring matter (red, yellow or blue pigment) should be added to the water so the difference between the plaster mold and the model cast in it can be easily told.

NOTE: If you wish to have an extra hard and lasting mold and one sure to be free from bubbles, use a resin mixed with water, one part resin to three parts water. (For the special resin needed, see Appendix C for suppliers.)

10. Pour plaster of paris into the bowl of water until it comes just slightly above the surface of the water and begins to form cracks like dried mud. A wet forefinger run around the edge of the bowl will take up the dry plaster that has settled there.

11. Mix the plaster and the water with a stick, spatula or old knife if the amount is small or with your hands if the amount is large. Mix very briefly until the plaster takes the form of a smooth and thick cream.

NOTE: Too much mixing is bad for the plaster. Don't take your hands or stick out of the mixture until you are finished stirring, as this forms air bubbles. Don't use a spoon, as this also makes bubbles.

12. Now pour an inch- to two-inch-thick layer of creamy plaster over the body of the animal in the box, blowing the plaster with your breath into all cracks and also blowing away all bubbles that may appear.

13. The plaster mold should be allowed to harden, which usually takes about half an hour.

14. To remove the animal after the plaster sets, turn the mold out of the box and set on a table bottom up. Remove the clay or cardboard pallet and pull the pins out by their points. Then carefully pull the animal out of the mold, cutting free any plaster that prevents this (see Figure 16e). Keep as much plaster in position as possible, as this will make a better cast later.

15. The plaster mold must now be thoroughly dried out before being used to make a model. This drying out should be at a temperature of from 90° to 105° F (32° to 41° C); over 105° causes the plaster to break down and become powdery).

The simplest way to do this is to place the mold in a small corrugated cardboard or wooden box with the top open. Put a lighted forty-watt electric light bulb into the top of this box and leave for at least twenty-four hours or until the mold is thoroughly dry. A regular homemade oven for drying out plaster molds can be made with a wooden box about $1 \times 1 \times 2$ feet in size. Make the top into a lid and drill six to twelve holes into it for ventilation. Line the inside of the box with fire-proof aluminum sheets and drill holes at both ends through which are stuck two forty-watt light bulbs. When lighted these heat up the oven. (See page 81 on how to make rubber models from this kind of plaster mold.)

Two-sided (or closed) plaster molds are sometimes necessary when the details of all sides of an animal must be shown. Figure 16f illustrates clearly all the steps to take in making such a two-sided mold. The main thing to remember is to use a plug of clay attached to the nose or the belly of the animal to make a funnel-shaped hole in the center of the mold. This funnel is later used for pouring in the casting material.

Making the Rubber Mold

The rubber mold is quite simple to make (as shown in Figure 17), but it usually needs to be backed by plaster of paris. Rubber molds are useful in catching delicate details, as in a flower, for example. Also, they are easier to take off a difficult subject after it has been set. Undercutting is not so important. A rubber mold can even be put completely around a subject and then cut in half or into several sections with scissors or a single-edge razor when it is set. (Turn to Appendix C at the end of this book for information on where to buy rubber molding compounds.) Rubber molds made from Rubber Anode Molding Compound are used mainly to make resin–wax models (see page 84). Plaster or stone may also be cast in rubber molds.

These are the steps for making a rubber mold:

1. The object to be placed in the mold—let us say it is a frog—is painted with liquid soap to prevent the rubber from sticking to it. This soap is allowed to dry.

NOTE: Some frogs, toads or salamanders may be so covered with mucus or slime that the soap will not be necessary.

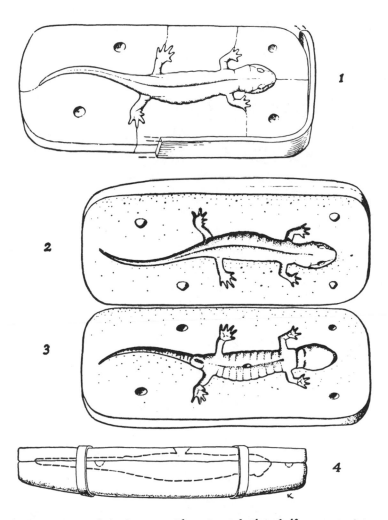

Fig. 16f. Two-sided plaster mold: (1) *clay is built up halfway around the animal, with "keyholes" cut in;* (2) *negative mold of top half, showing the raised "keys"; the animal is placed in it to cast the bottom half* (3), *in which a pouring hole is made;* (4) *the two sides are banded together for pouring.*

Fig.17. Making a rubber mold of a frog or toad, in three sections.

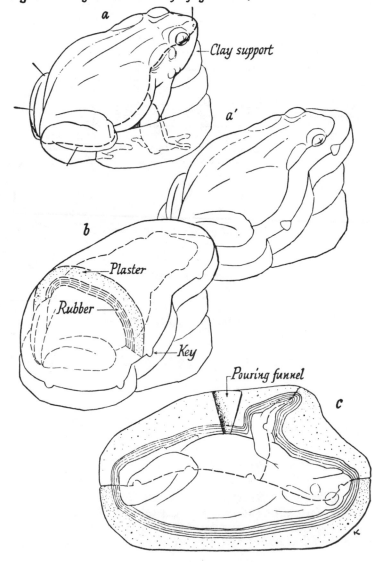

2. The frog's body and legs are covered one-half the way up with clay, and the animal is pinned with headless pins to this clay. An even rim of clay is made around the body and in this flat rim, holes (shaped like half-circles) are punched to help in later joining the two half-molds together (see Figure 17a).
3. If the rubber molding material is not creamy and smooth enough to use easily, it may be mixed with water. Mixing is best done by adding water (up to 50 percent), then allowing to stand overnight in a closed container. This makes the material become quite liquid. Warming in a double boiler will help hasten this process.
4. The rubber composition is painted onto the uncovered half of the frog with a brush, brushing outward from the center.

NOTE: This brush must first have been soaked in liquid soap, squeezed between the fingers, and the soap allowed to dry in the inner part of the brush. This stops the rubber from getting into the brush.

Brush over every part carefully. Wash brush afterward.
5. When this first coat has set enough—in about fifteen minutes—another layer is brushed on. This is kept up until the covering is about ¼ to ½ inch thick. This hardens soon into the first half-mold. A mother mold of plaster of paris must then be put on the back of the rubber mold to give it strength (see Figure 17b).
6. The clay is taken away from the other half of the frog, and the edge of the first half-mold is shellacked (or liquid soap used) so it will not stick to the second. This is allowed to dry.
7. The second half-mold is brushed over the untouched side of the frog as described above, and allowed to harden. When hard, the two half-molds (within their mother plaster-of-paris molds) are pulled off the frog.
8. A funnel-shaped opening is always left at one end of the mold. Into this opening the material for making the model is to be poured. It is made by using a plug of clay shaped like a funnel and touching the point of the plug to a good place on the belly of the frog (see Figure 17c).

For details on making plaster or wax models in this rubber mold see pages 80 and 84.

Making the Plaster Positive or Final Model

A plaster model or cast can be made from either a plaster mold or a rubber mold. It is usually more easily made from a rubber mold as this flexible material can have undercuts on the model and yet still be pulled off. One drawback to a plaster model is that it breaks easily.

NOTE: For protecting plaster against breakage, use the special resin mentioned on page 75. If used in a museum display, the plaster model must be placed in a position where it will not be easily broken. Another drawback is that if there are undercuts, or parts of the mold where the animal's body curves under the mold surface, then a plaster model must be pulled out very carefully or it will be easily broken. Plaster models should thus be used in plaster molds only when the mold has an open face from which the model can easily be removed.

Follow the steps below when making a plaster model:

1. The inside of the mold is washed with liquid soap or shellac so that a thin film is left on the surface. This is allowed to dry. It then prevents the model or cast from sticking to the mold.
2. If a closed mold is used, the two halves of the mold are bound together with stout rubber bands. They should fit together as perfectly as possible, and have a funnel-shaped hole at one end for pouring the casting material (as illustrated in Figure 17c).
3. The plaster mix is made as described on pages 73 and 75.
4. It is poured slowly in through the funnel opening in the closed mold, and the mold is turned from side to side so that the liquid plaster will run to all parts and will not form air pockets. In an open or one-sided mold the plaster is poured in until it completely fills the hole.
5. When the mold is filled with plaster it is allowed to set, preferably in a dry place under a small amount of heat.
6. When set, the cast is removed from the mold, and is then heated for at least twenty-four hours in from 90° to 105° F (32° to 41° C) heat. It is then ready for painting and mounting (see page 95).

Making the Rubber Positive
or Final Model

In Appendix C you are told where to obtain a rubber molding material for making rubber molds. This same material can be used for making the positive model inside either a plaster-of-paris open-faced (one-sided) mold or a closed (or two-sided) mold. Another rubber material also good for this job is described in the second half of this section. It is often easiest in making museum displays to use one-sided models of lizards, snakes, frogs or salamanders. These one-sided models are placed face down on a platform of moss or on a rock or on sand where they appear just as lifelike as they would if made in two-sided or closed molds.

The following steps should be taken to make a rubber one-sided model:

1. The plaster mold should have been made as described on pages 72–76; in other words, covering more than half of the animal's body and all of its head. With a rubber model, it is all right if there is some undercutting of the body inside the mold, as the rubber is elastic and easily removed. No soap or other separating agent need be placed in the mold, since the rubber molding compound pulls free easily. Even the breaking of a plaster mold need not worry you, as a very fine cast or model will still be the result.
2. Thin the rubber compound to a creamy state (as described on page 79) and pour into a *dry* mold. The plaster withdraws water from the rubber compound nearest it and sets up a "wall." Keep the mold filled with rubber compound until the wall or rubber nearest the plaster is thick enough ($\frac{1}{16}$ to $\frac{1}{4}$ inch). Be sure the latex or rubber reaches even the tips of the toes by gently rocking the mold to swish the rubber into every detail. After the wall is made pour back into the container any extra liquid.
3. Let the mold set in a warm, dry area for about twenty-four hours. Sprinkle talcum powder on the rubber cast inside the mold and remove by pulling gently (see Figure 18).
4. If needed (as with fish) the cast can be filled later with foam plastic block, balsa-wood block or plaster. When the plaster filler is set, remove it to dry and then put it back inside the body of the model.
5. Wash the film of plaster from the outside of the cast or

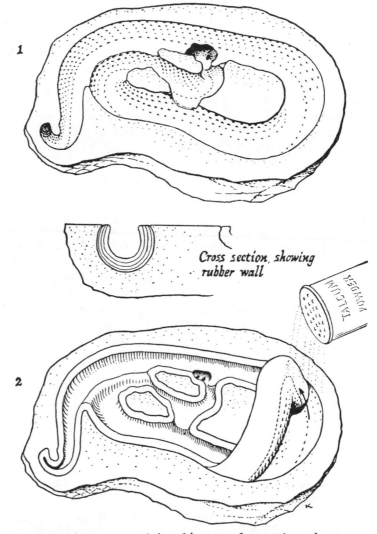

Cross section, showing
rubber wall

TALCUM POWDER

*Fig. 18.(1) Plaster one-sided mold (example, a sidewinder);
(2) pulling rubber cast out of mold, using talcum powder.*

model. Paint with thin shellac and dry. Next paint the model with artists' oils to make it appear like the original or live specimen and let dry. More surface shellac may be needed to give a glossy finish. (Other details on painting are given on pages 95–96.)

6. Either after or before painting, any excess rubber should be trimmed away with scissors until the model is natural in appearance.

7. If any imperfections are found in the outer part of the cast or model, they can be easily fixed. Any projections should be cut away with a sharp razor. Hollows are carefully painted over with the liquid rubber molding compound until they are correctly filled.

8. Eyes on small casts can be painted. Glass or plastic eyes may be needed in fish (small beads or buttons can be used).

9. The specimen is ready for use in an exhibit. Don't squeeze it, as the paint may crack and pop off.

To make a closed model of an animal or plant either the above or the following rubber molding compound may be used. The new material is called Air Cure Flexible Slip (see Appendix C for a source of this material). It is excellent for making accurate casts of animals and may be used in either open-faced or closed molds. But it is not so flexible or so easily removed from a mold as Rubber Anode Molding Compound. Flexible Slip is a milklike liquid made largely of water. The secret of using it in a plaster mold is to draw off the water quickly so that the rubber material soon sets into a hard and durable model or cast.

The steps below should be taken to make a model or cast in a closed mold with Air Cure Flexible Slip (similar steps are used with the Rubber Anode Molding Compound first described).

NOTE: If suppliers have other materials for casting than those named, ask them to furnish materials with similar or better qualities, and furnish instructions for use.

1. The plaster mold should be completely freed from all moisture by keeping it in from 90° to 105° F (32° to 41° C) heat for at least twenty-four hours (as described on page 75 in this chapter). The two halves of the plaster mold must each be at least 1 inch thick, better even thicker.

2. The Flexible Slip should be stirred thoroughly so it is like a free-flowing cream. If necessary more water can be stirred into it to make it sufficiently free flowing.

3. The two halves of the mold should be firmly bound together with all parts joined exactly by heavy rubber bands. One end should have a funnel-shaped opening to receive the Slip (see Figure 16f).

4. *No soap or other agent is necessary to separate the cast from the mold.* You now pour the Flexible Slip directly into the mold through the funnel opening. Pour slowly, a small amount at a time. Use a nail or small stick to keep the hole at the bottom of the funnel open. Rock the mold from side to side to get the Flexible Slip into all parts of the mold and get rid of air pockets. Pour until the mold will take no more Slip. If the mold is warm when the Slip is poured into it, this will help the cast to set more quickly. The liquid in the Slip will be absorbed (pulled away) by the dry plaster in the mold. Keep the mold filled for from six to twenty minutes until you are sure there is enough wall thickness in the cast.

5. In about twelve hours, if you leave the mold in an ordinary room, you can remove the cast or model from the mold. First pour any extra Slip back into the container. At the same time wipe away all overflow Slip from the edges of each half-mold with a piece of newspaper. This helps free the cast from the mold, as otherwise it may stick and break apart in coming out. Do not try to take the cast out of the mold until it is firm enough to come out as one piece. The setting of the mold can be hurried by putting the mold under a forty-watt lamp in a small box at 105° F (41° C).

6. Allow the cast or model to dry fully before trying to paint.

7. A water-soluble dye can be added to the Flexible Slip before pouring into the mold to give the cast or model any color you wish. If the animal has a general brown ground color, for example, then it would be wise to mix brown dye with the Slip used. Other colors can be painted on over this as desired.

Making the Resin–Wax Positive or Final Model

Resin–wax models are harder to make than those made of rubber or plaster and often require more training. However, such beautiful results can often be had with these models that they are well worth experimenting with. Flowers and leaves, for example, can be made so perfectly as to appear almost exactly like the real thing. A person who becomes expert in the job of making these can develop an interesting sideline business.

Resin–wax molding material can be purchased ready-made through your dentist from his or her dental supply house or sometimes through your doctor, who can get such material from a medical supply house. A drugstore also may have a source of supply. It is cheaper, however, to make your own mixture, the parts of which can usually be bought at local stores (particularly drug and hardware stores). The following two formulas are recommended by Professor Carl D. Clarke in his book *Molding and Casting*. The first formula is used for brushing into open molds. It is particularly good for very delicate work where all the parts of a flower, for example, must be shown. The second formula is for pouring rather than brushing into a mold. This second mixture is good for most ordinary purposes.

Formula Number 1, for brushing into molds, is as follows:

Ingredients	*Parts by weight*
"Parawax" (paraffin; 133° F or 56° C)	5 oz
Resin (colophony, bleached)	8 oz
Light carnauba wax	1 oz
Talc	2 oz
Zinc oxide	¼ oz

Melt the carnauba wax and the paraffin together in a double boiler. Then mix in the resin by stirring until the resin and wax are thoroughly mixed together. Next stir in the talc and then the zinc oxide until a smooth creamy mixture appears. If there is any frothing or bubbling, remove the mixture from the stove and stir in a few drops of benzene (be careful, as benzene catches fire if spilled on a stove). The mixture can be colored by putting a small amount of melted wax in a tablespoon and mixing it carefully with the coloring matter. Then use the spoon to stir the color into the main batch of melted wax. Ground colors of animals are put on in this way, whereas other colors of the design may be put on afterward with a brush.

Formula Number 2, for pouring into molds, is as follows:

Ingredients	*Parts by weight*
"Parawax" or paraffin	8 oz
Carnauba wax (light)	2 oz
Beeswax (yellow)	1 oz
Resin (bleached)	2 oz
Turpentine or benzene	1½ drams

First melt and mix the waxes in a double boiler. Then mix in the resin by stirring vigorously. Do not put the turpentine or benzene in until the pot is removed from the stove, as otherwise the benzene may catch fire. It is while the wax is in a melted state but cool enough to be touched with the hand that it should be poured into the mold.

The steps in making a resin–wax model are:

1. Paint the interior of the mold or half-molds with a thin layer of liquid soap. This prevents the resin–wax from sticking to the mold. Allow to dry.
2. If the mold has many small corners to it and looks difficult to fill, use Formula Number 1 above for your resin–wax mixture. Brush the warm liquid mixture into the open half-molds or the mold with a camel's-hair brush. After the wax hardens into a thin layer, continue as explained below.
3. If the mold is not a difficult one, you can skip the above step 2 and instead pour resin–wax mixture Number 2 into a mold. If it is a double mold bound together with rubber bands, the liquid is poured in through the funnel-shaped opening at one end (see Figure 17c). Pour a small quantity in first and swish the mold around until you feel sure all corners have been covered. Pour the remainder of the wax back into your container (which is kept warm in a double boiler) and allow that inside the mold to harden a bit before pouring the next layer.
4. When the cast is about ⅛ inch thick, it should be reinforced with a layer of gauze. The gauze (cut to size) should first be dipped into the hot wax mixture to thoroughly saturate it. Then lay it in the mold. The closed mold must be opened for this job, and then closed again. In the open mold simply add the gauze (or cotton) to each layer of wax as poured. Such gauze or cotton reinforcements prevent easy breakage of the model. Each piece of gauze (two or three layers can be used) should be carefully brushed out smooth in the cast with a varnish brush.
5. When the resin–wax hardens, the mold may be opened and the cast or model removed. You must look it over carefully for bad parts. Anything sticking out from the mold that should not be there should be trimmed off with a single-edged razor. If there is a place on the mold that needs filling, you may fix it by dipping a brush in the warm liquid resin–wax mixture and then brushing it carefully over the hollow until it is filled. This soon hardens.

6. How to paint the model is described on page 95. How to make models of leaves and flowers is described in the next two sections. How to mount the models in a museum display is described in Chapter 9.

How to Make Resin–Wax Models of Leaves and Flowers

Reproducing leaves and flowers is a difficult job and takes some practicing. But very beautiful examples can be made by a careful worker. The tools shown in Figure 19a are needed and can be purchased from any biological supply company (see Appendix C).

The following steps are taken in making a resin–wax model of a leaf:

1. The leaf should be soaked in 5 percent formalin solution to preserve it.
2. After you have made the original mold of the leaf in plaster or rubber, melt the resin–wax molding material (Formula Number 1) in a double boiler.

NOTE: The same mold may be used over and over.

3. Paint each of the two halves of the mold of the leaf with the resin–wax mixture, using a camel's-hair brush. Allow this first thin coat to partly harden.
4. Meanwhile, a bundle of thin wires should have been tapered by dipping them in a bottle of nitric acid and slowly pulling them out. One of these wires is used as the midrib of the leaf. Cut it to size and place it on the first wax coat so that it will be like the true leaf rib, with one end serving as the leaf stem. This stem part should be left long enough so that it may be wrapped around the main stem of the model plant-to-be.
5. Dip a layer of gauze or cotton cut to fit the shape of the leaf in the warm wax and then place this layer in one half of the mold.
6. Paint the resin–wax on both halves of the mold until the thickness is about the same as the original leaf. Then press and tie the two halves of the mold together as shown in Figure 19b. The plaster or rubber mold should be soaked in hot water to keep the wax from chilling and to allow easy separation of the wax from the plaster.
7. After about an hour and a half to let the cast set, open the

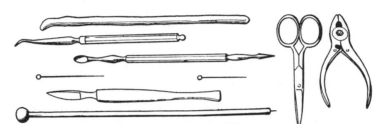

(a) Tools needed for making resin-wax flowers (after Am. Mus. Nat. Hist.)

Fig. 19.

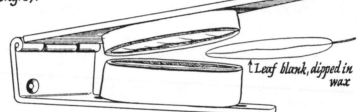

↑Leaf blank, dipped in wax

(b) Squeeze mold for a leaf, made with a large strap hinge, plaster molds

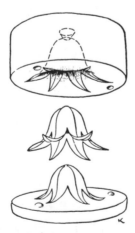

(c) Trimming the molded leaf with the scissors

(d) A plaster mold for a calyx. Note pouring hole in the top.

mold up and take the model out. Trim it with scissors until it takes its natural shape (see Figure 19c).

8. The leaf may now be wired or glued onto a stem made of wire coated with resin–wax to proper thickness, and so made part of an entire plant, modeled from life. (How to use the wooden stems of plants is explained in the next section.) Very complicated leaves, such as the leaf of the pitcher plant, are best cast in rubber.

Making flowers is more difficult than making leaves. Each petal of the flower usually has to be molded separately, though it is sometimes possible to make a rubber mold of the entire flower. The sepal cup (calyx) or each sepal by itself should also be made in separate molds (see Figure 19d). The pistil is made by running the wax-coated wire stem through the center of the wax flower, the other parts of which have been assembled in their proper places and attached with hot wax. Wax of the proper color should then be molded around the wire tip in a shape similar to that in life. The wax mixture may be handled in the hands at a temperature of about 120° F (49° C). Test with a thermometer or simply use the wax when it cools enough not to burn the fingers. The stamens are made of thread or of brush bristles tipped with yellow wax. When leaves and flowers have been properly linked together with wire and wax they form a spray of the plant or even a whole plant. This must be carefully painted in natural colors and set up in a museum exhibit.

Some Other Ways to Make Plant Models

Mushrooms should be done in two pieces (see Figure 20). Cut the stem off from the top where they connect and form two half-molds of plaster around the top. Make the funnel or pouring hole where the stem was cut off from the top (see page 76). Into this double mold either rubber compound or resin–wax can be poured to make the model. The stem should be separately pushed, cut end down, into soft plaster. The gills under the heads of mushrooms are often hard to get in detail. If you want best results with the gills, use a rubber mold. But a plaster mold may give all the detail you want, particularly if in your museum display you turn the gill side of your mushroom away from the watcher. If both parts of the mushroom are made out of rubber molding material in a plaster mold, then the model stem should be attached to the model top with a spot of fresh

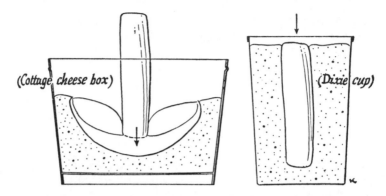

Fig.20. Making plaster molds of mushroom umbrella and stem.

rubber compound. If you want to show the gills of a mushroom in your exhibit, then the original mold must be made with the funnel opening entering the top of the mushroom "umbrella." Then in the exhibit that side should be turned away from the watcher.

Here are some rules of plant construction:

First rule: Carefully look over *every* detail of the live plant you wish to make a model of. Take a petal and later a leaf and hold it alone, studying every detail of texture, color, thickness, hairyness, where it is attached and so on.

Second rule: Use any woody or other natural parts that will not shrink, wilt, rot or otherwise change (for example, the dried leaves at the lower end of a stem). Don't try to make a model of anything that you can use exactly as it is in nature.

Third rule: Let the job at hand help you decide the materials to be used. If it is a very difficult flower or leaf you wish to make a model of, it is probably better to make a rubber mold completely around it, then cut the mold after it hardens into sections. If you have a wooden stem, use that in your exhibit and attach model leaves and flowers to it by wire and cement. And so on.

Fourth rule: Wherever possible, use a real plant or plant parts as a color guide.

Fleshy plants like rock lettuce or cacti can be molded in plaster and cast in rubber. Cut the fleshy part of the cluster away from the

dry basal parts. Separate the leaves and stick each, point first, in soft
plaster of paris leaving the butt end barely exposed. When the plaster sets, dry over warm air until the leaves are nearly crisp. Take out
leaves and pour in creamlike rubber molding compound (as described on page 81). Keep holes filled until no more rubber is absorbed. Set aside in a warm spot for twenty-four to thirty-six hours.
Sprinkle talcum powder on the exposed rubber surface and pull the
rubber "leaves" by force from the mold. Shellac the rubber and let
dry. Then paint with artists' oils and allow to dry. You can shellac
the leaves a second time if a shiny color is needed. Now join the
leaves together again (using the rubber compound as cement) as
they were in the original plant. Place this manufactured part of the
plant back in the natural woody base part which you kept (see Figure 21). The flowering stalk can be made up like other soft stems and
blossoms, as described below.

For a woody plant with soft leaves and new growth, the leaves
can be cut from crepe paper or noncrepe papers such as paper towels
or rice paper or even wrapping paper. If the leaf is somewhat heavy,
as with manzanita and some lilies, you can cut the leaves in large
numbers from paper folded into several layers, using a pattern and
scissors. Attach a wire stem to the leaf with model-airplane glue or
the cellulose cement described below. Dip the leaf into a latex-base

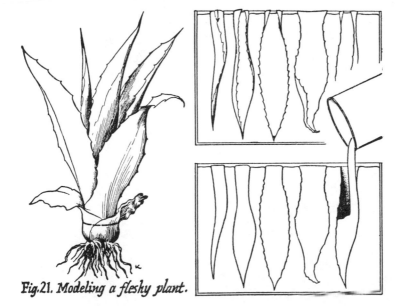

Fig. 21. Modeling a fleshy plant.

paint (bought at a hardware store). Primary colors of these paints can be mixed together to produce secondary colors. For example, yellow and blue mixed make green. If you wish to add overtones later, dip the leaf in colored shellac. Shiny surfaces can be produced with shellac; dull ones with a flat varnish or a varnish with fine pumice added. Oil colors can be dulled by mixing in talcum powder. Only experimenting with different methods will show you what is best for each job.

Build up the petiole (leaf stem) and other soft stems by wrapping cotton on the wire with your fingers dipped in a cellulose–acetate solution (see Figure 22a). This solution is made by dissolving shredded sheet cellulose-acetate in acetone. (These substances may usually be purchased through your drugstore.) Thickness should be determined by the needs of the problem and more acetate or more acetone can always be added. When the wrapped stem is dry, any desired paint can be used over it. Stems are best built up by twisting each leaf stem or petiole about the main stem until all the leaves are attached to the stem as they were in life.

Thinner leaves can easily be made up of one or two layers of thin paper cut to shape, cemented on or together (depending on whether one or two layers are used) over a wire center vein which

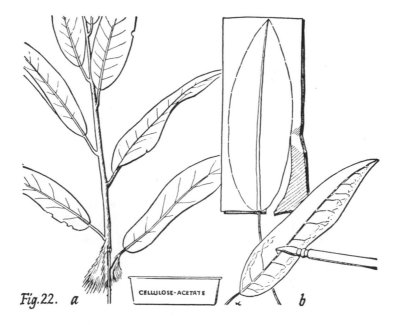

Fig. 22. *a*   CELLULOSE-ACETATE   *b*

sticks out at the leaf base as the petiole. More leaf veining can be put on later by laying the leaf on a blotter and using a nutpick, dental tool or a nail to make lines on the leaf (see Figure 22b).

Size and other variations in leaves cut from one pattern can be made by cutting defects or missing areas with scissors. Such defects must be *faithfully* reproduced in the final color, too. For example, if a discolored brown area is around a defect in a leaf, show it.

Flower petals are made up of paper material most suited to the purpose which has been dipped in the cellulose-acetate and acetone mixture (see Figure 23). An excellent color material for small shiny petals is model-airplane dope. This dope blends well into many colors using just the primary colors—red, yellow and blue—plus black and white. It dries quickly and can be overlaid with other colors later if desired.

An airbrush is good to have for color blending, but is too expensive for most people. A thin wash of little color and much medium (shellac, varnish, oil or turpentine) will often do a good job of blending. Multicolors and color depth can be had by painting on several layers of this thin wash with a camel's-hair brush, allowing each coat to dry before putting on a new one.

Carefully study and meet each problem as it comes up. You will be surprised how easy it is to overcome difficulties in this work with just a little thinking and experimenting. For example, stamens and pistils can be built up of wire, cotton and cellulose-acetate or string plus liquid latex and paint, or bristles (nylon brushes have good bristles for this job) and paint.

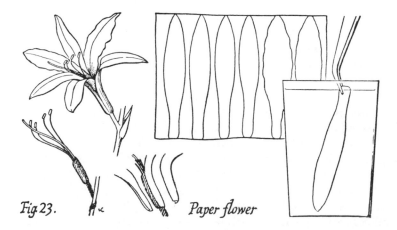

Fig 23.   *Paper flower*

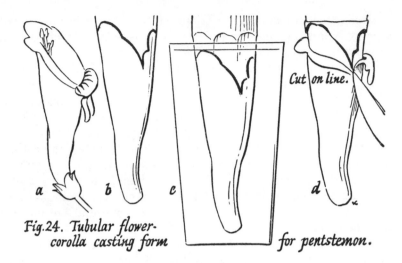

Fig.24. Tubular flower-corolla casting form for pentstemon.

Tubular flower-corolla casting forms for such flowers as pent-stemon, monkey flower or daffodil (Figure 24a) can be cut from wax or soft wood covered with wax. This form should have the outer corolla edge lines well marked (Figure 24b). Dip the form, ovary end first, into thin liquid rubber molding compound (Figure 24c) up to the desired level and then dry. Keep this up until enough thickness is obtained for the model flower. The model can be rubbed with tal-cum powder, rolled off the form (Figure 24d), reversed and colored as described above. Then it is ready to be put together with the other parts of the plant, using wires and cement.

Cellulose-acetate and acetone mixture can be used in place of the thin liquid latex as described above. A thin slit cut with a razor down one side will help you take the acetate off the corolla casting form and the model can be mended with a touch of acetone.

Fuzzy leaves, fruit, stems and so forth can be made by putting on after painting some silk or cotton flock (obtained from a drug-store), genuine peach fuzz or genuine plant hairs. This fuzz can be sifted over the model while the paint or shellac is still wet.

The fleshy seaweeds have been successfully done in one-piece plaster molds, rubbing thick Rubber Anode Molding Compound (see Appendix C) by hand into the mold, or pouring a thinner compound if you wish. Since the seaweeds are mounted by glue or cement on a rock, the appearance of the underside is not important. Spray shel-lac (try an ordinary fly sprayer) over the rubber to protect it from the oil colors which are added next. A second coat of shellac over the paint makes the surface of the seaweed look as wet as if the sea had just left it.

Meaty fruits such as cherries and grapes can be built up of the cellulose-acetate mixture and cotton. Berries can be molded in a one-piece plaster mold and cast by pouring the wax or the rubber molding compound through where the stem opening of the fruit normally is. Or a rubber mold and a wax model may be used. Larger fruits, such as apples and peaches, are best done in two-piece molds, pouring the wax or rubber compound in through the stem end. Be sure to keep the mold full so the material reaches all areas equally. A stem of wire, cotton and cellulose-acetate, or a genuine wooden stem will fill most of the pouring hole left after casting. If not, build and shape up an accurate plug of thick rubber molding compound around the stem. (Fruits may also be carved out of soft balsa wood.)

Heavy ferns (such as bracken) can be partly taken apart and each branch pressed *lightly* between newspapers or thick, soft cardboard until half dry. Then paint each branch *on both surfaces* with a latex-base paint. If correct paint is used, no more needs to be done except a light spraying of shellac in about two days. The parts can then be put together again on wire, cotton and cellulose-acetate stems which are then properly painted. A touch-up with a thin color wash or spray is a good idea to get a lighter color near the branch tips and to mark the undersides with the brown or gold of spore patches.

Grasses (except the young green grasses) may be preserved by dipping them in a solution of one part each of glycerine and formalin and eight parts of water. You then mount them in your exhibit by sticking them in the dirt or in holes bored in papier-mâché. However, the preserving changes their colors, so they need to be painted lightly with oil colors to give them a natural appearance again.

Some half-dry plants, such as grasses, cattails, and so forth, can be preserved a long time by spraying them with liquid plastic. (Spray cans of plastic can be bought or ordered at your local hardware store.)

Further Information on Coloring Models

It is necessary to color the plaster, rubber, resin–wax or acetate models as closely as possible to their colors in real life. This takes some experience and practice before good jobs are done, though some simple things, such as leaves and stems, color rather easily.

Most models need to be painted with shellac first and allowed to dry. This protects the surface from the action of paints.

There are two main ways to color your models. One is by mixing a color right into the molding mixture (as described on page 84). The other is to paint everything on with a brush from the outside. Since many things look more natural if they have deep color as well as surface color, it is wise to learn how to color right into the material. In the cast of a lizard, for example, if its general color is brown, then the molding mixture of which the cast is made should be colored brown. Afterwards the other colors can be put on the outside with a brush wherever they belong.

Transparent oil colors used for painting photographs are often good for painting resin–wax, plaster or rubber models. A set of these may be bought at any art goods store. Also water and tempera colors can be used for painting some models. Lacquers and enamel colors give a beautiful glossy effect to a model. Even fingernail enamel can be so used. Use good quality small brushes if you wish to get the best effect. And experiment with different types of coloring materials to see which are best. (It is always possible that other types of paints will also do a good job, and may be worth experimenting with. Try acrylic paints, for example.)

If oils or lacquers are used on a resin–wax cast, the cast should be painted first with a very light coat of white shellac. This helps prevent details from being lost.

Paint should be put on a model in very thin coats, as otherwise the paint will hide the details. The reason transparent oil colors are good is that they color without hiding.

When painting your model, have the natural object in front of you if possible to use as an example of the right colors. If it is an animal, it should be freshly killed or alive. If a plant, it should be freshly picked and kept in water. Otherwise try to get a color picture to copy from. Your last resort is to color from a description in a book.

After the paint on the model dries, your work is ready to be fitted into the museum exhibit. (See Chapter 9.)

Books that may give you further help in your painting work are listed in Appendix B.

THE USE OF PAPIER-MÂCHÉ

Papier-mâché is often used for landscapes in museum scenes, either miniature or life-size, and also for miniature models of such things as volcanoes, glaciers and rock formations, usually showing a cross section of a portion of the earth's surface. It may even be used to take the place of the bark of a tree or for making artificial rock. It is very durable, and if you paint it carefully or glue dirt or sand to it, it becomes quite realistic. It is also easy to make.

A formular for papier-mâché used by the American Museum of Natural History is as follows:

> Felt building paper
> Dextrine
> Whiting
> Plaster of paris

The paper is torn in shreds and macerated [ground up] in water. The dextrine is mixed in cold water to the consistency of thin syrup. Equal parts of plaster and whiting are mixed together dry. Take equal parts of damp paper and plaster-whiting mixture and add dextrine syrup [until like a thick paste]. This mixture if applied as a thick paste should set in less than an hour. To hasten the setting, add more plaster and dextrine.

Be sure to make enough papier-mâché for whatever size job you have to do. While it is still in the paste-like form, it must be molded in the hands (as you would clay) into whatever shape you desire. You can make it into a tree trunk, a miniature mountain, or a boulder, or a miniature hill, or the sloping land surrounding a miniature lake. If you wish to show a cross section of a mountain, a volcano, etc., you must build up your mountain or other formation against a flat board and then take away the board when the papier-mâché hardens. Two boards nailed together at right angles will give you a cross section on two sides if your papier-mâché is built into this corner in the shape desired.

After the papier-mâché has set, it must be painted in the natural colors of the scenery shown. Either oil or watercolor paints can be used, or enamel if a gloss is desired. Papier-mâché can be partially waterproofed by mixing in with it the whites of eggs or some sulphate of iron.

MOUNTING MODELS ON BOARDS

Models of plaster are wired to board mounts as described for rocks on pages 44–45. But wax and rubber models may usually be glued or cemented to the boards wherever desired. Use of models in museum displays is described in Chapter 9.

SOME LAST SUGGESTIONS ABOUT MODEL MAKING

Some people have worked most of their lives making models for museums, but even these experts are still learning new tricks of the trade. You can experiment with the methods described here, but there are many other ways to try. Some books listed in Appendix B will describe some of these other ways. Still others you can discover yourself with a little experimenting, a little imagination and a little patience.

Here are a few suggestions of things to try:

- If you are good at clay modeling or soap carving, you can make many figures for your museum out of these materials. This is especially true of miniature scenes, such as one showing an ancient Indian cliff dwelling. The cliff and buildings can be modeled in clay. The human and animal figures can either be modeled out of clay or carved out of soap.
- If you are not good at modeling or sculpturing, you can still make such miniature scenes by the art of model casting already described. Molded miniature figures of men or animals can be found at many a five-and-ten store, art store, or borrowed from a friend. From these you can make your own plaster or rubber molds and then out of the molds make plaster, rubber or wax duplicates. If the wax casts are taken out of their molds while still warm, the limbs of animals and men can be turned in different directions as desired. For example, you can take the figure of a woman and make it kneel as if it were an American Indian woman grinding corn.
- For some scenes, paper or cardboard models can be made. The art of paper modeling is described in *Paper Constructions* by Franz Zeier listed in Appendix B under "Models and Modeling."
- Plastics of all kinds from Plexiglas to Bakelite can be cut, carved or molded into models you can use for miniature scenes. Insects and other small creatures can be mounted inside transparent plastic blocks by placing them in liquid plastic set in forms and allowing the plastic to harden. Plastic laminating can be applied to thin objects such as pressed plant specimens, giving them a protective coat that probably will last for centuries. Most large cities have hobby stores

where information about this work can be obtained. Books listed in Appendix B give information on working plastics.

- Soft wood (especially balsa wood) can be cut, sawed, carved, filed and sandpapered into many shapes for use in museum displays. Books listed in Appendix B give help in this work.
- Model lakes or other bodies of water in a miniature scene can be made by using blue-tinted sheets of glass or plastic cut to shape and supported by papier-mâché.
- Blood can be imitated by using red enamal fingernail polish.
- Miniature trees can be made by using sticks of soft wood lined with small nail holes in which are stuck green pine or fir needles. As the needles fade in color, paint them green. Other types of trees can be made by using rough paper (like paper toweling) and cutting it into the proper shapes. Glue the paper to stick "trunks," cement to your miniature scene, and paint them the proper colors.
- Sand can be painted different colors to show water, hills, farm land, desert and so forth. Thin poster paint poured or sprayed over the sand will do.
- A green-tinted transparent plastic sheet placed in front of an undersea scene gives a fine feeling of realism.

8

Drawings, Charts, Diagrams and Paintings

Most people don't know their own ability or what they like or don't like until they have tried something new. In this regard I am always reminded of my son Kirby when he was about nine. He told me very strongly one day at lunch that he didn't like a new dish we had just cooked, an old Dutch dish called "bread, potato and eggs." "Why, Kirby," I said, "you haven't even tasted it!" "But I know I won't like it," came the reply. "Well, try it anyway." Finally he agreed to taste some. At first taste a beautiful look of pleasure came over his face, and he ate up two helpings in a hurry!

You may never have done much drawing, but until you have really practiced it awhile you can hardly be said to know what you can do. Diagrams, of course, can be made with a pencil and a ruler, and anybody who can hold a pencil steady and use a little intelligence can draw a diagram. This chapter cannot, of course, teach you how to draw. That job is for books that spend all their space on the subject. But it can suggest ways and means to use drawings, charts, diagrams and paintings in preparing your nature museum. Such art work does not need to be your own. It can be done by a friend or partner who has ability, or you can trace or enlarge drawings, diagrams and charts you find in books and magazines. You can even have photostats of such drawings and diagrams made by a commercial blueprint company and enlarged to any size you want. This is particularly useful when you want to have a very large copy of a drawing, diagram or chart you find in a book.

DRAWINGS FOR YOUR MUSEUM DISPLAYS

In doing research for a museum display you often run across drawings in a magazine or book that you think would be useful in your display. For example, in a magazine you might find a drawing of the inside of a termite nest and want to use this drawing in a display of the life of termites.

You can, of course, copy such a drawing directly by tracing it on tracing paper. But usually for a wall museum display you will want to enlarge such a drawing until it will easily be seen and understood by a visitor coming into your room. You can, as already suggested, take the book or magazine to a blueprint shop and have them make an enlarged copy of the drawing for you. You can also use a Contoura and have your Contoura print enlarged.*

On the other hand you may wish to make an enlarged copy of the drawing by hand. There is one way to do this that is very simple and easy for a beginner who has had no experience in art work. Take a sheet of transparent tracing paper and with a pencil draw squares on it about ½ inch in diameter. Place the paper with the squares over the drawing you wish to copy and enlarge. Stick it lightly to the page with masking tape. Now take another and larger sheet of regular drawing paper and draw squares on it. If you wish to enlarge the picture two times, make the squares ¾ inch in diameter. If you wish to enlarge four times, make the squares 1 inch in diameter. And so on (see Figure 25).

Your next job is to fill the large squares on your drawing paper with the same lines that are found in each of the smaller squares in the original drawing. With a little care and with far greater ease than you could make such a drawing freehand you will soon have a good enlarged copy of what you want. Now ink the lines of your drawing, but leave the lines of the squares in pencil. As soon as the ink is dried, these pencil lines should be erased. An art gum eraser is best for this purpose. If possible, you can then paint your copy of the drawing with a good set of watercolors and have a beautiful and instructive addition to your museum display. This painting should be done either from life or from a colored picture of the object in a

---

* Write F. G. Ludwig Associates, Pease Road, Woodbridge, CT 06525, for information about the Contoura, or ask about it at your nearest university library.

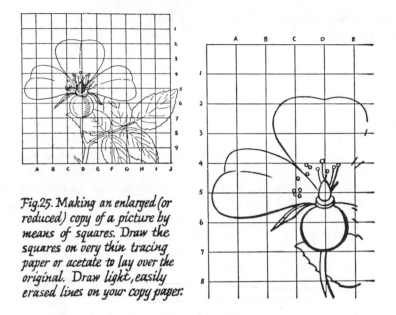

Fig.25. Making an enlarged (or reduced) copy of a picture by means of squares. Draw the squares on very thin tracing paper or acetate to lay over the original. Draw light, easily erased lines on your copy paper.

book. Take your time, carefully trying to get the colors as exact as possible.

It may be that you are a sufficiently good artist to make your own freehand drawings of things you wish to show in your museum display. Even a beginner can make good drawings of very simple things, especially if they are at all diagrammatic. For example, even if you know little about art, you can make a drawing of a cross section of an ant nest as you expose the nest when you cut into its side with a pick and shovel. Cross sections of the insides of plants or mountains (as for instance in a highway cut) are also easy for the beginner to draw. If you paint your drawings neatly in natural colors, this greatly adds to their attractiveness.

DIAGRAMS AND CHARTS

Diagrams and charts are more likely to be used in your museum display than drawings. They are extremely useful in showing a whole story about something in one glance, especially if they are well done. Plans 2 and 5 show examples of both a diagram and a chart as used in museum displays (Plan 5 is on page 114). Both diagrams and charts are drawn with tools such as rulers, squares, drawing compasses and protractors. Therefore they can be made by people who have no artistic ability, although the work must be done carefully and neatly. (Some good books on mechanical drawing are listed in Appendix B.)

It is wise to study diagrams and charts as used in books to help you in deciding how to make your own diagrams and charts. Often you can use a diagram or chart exactly as it is in a book if it is on the subject of your museum display. For example, suppose you are telling the story of how necessary flesh-eating animals are in keeping plant-eating animals from getting too numerous. The very simple diagram shown in Figure 26 could easily be enlarged to handsomely illustrate your museum display, using the method of enlarging given on pages 101–102.

When making diagrams or charts, whether your own or copies or enlargements, remember that they must be large enough to be clearly seen and understood by your visitors. Keep your lettering large enough to be easily read. Use contrasting colors to help bring out the ideas shown in the chart or diagram more clearly. Use colors, however, that contrast harmoniously. Blue and red, for example, do not contrast well, nor do green and orange.

Pictures of animals and plants done as simple black silhouettes

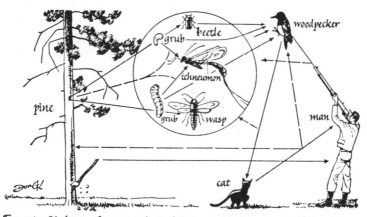

Fig. 26. Linkage of many ecological factors. EXPLANATION: Solid lines connect aggressor and his victim, arrows pointing to beneficiary of action. Broken lines with arrows point to indirect beneficiary of aggression – e.g.: man kills woodpecker; insects benefit. Man kills cat; woodpecker and tree benefit. Note that man gains nothing by killing insect-eating bird, but loses tree to insects.

REPTILE LIFE IN THE DESERT

↑ *Tell the story on a neat label*

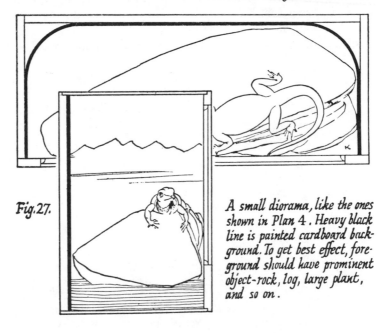

Fig. 27.

A small diorama, like the ones shown in Plan 4. Heavy black line is painted cardboard background. To get best effect, foreground should have prominent object-rock, log, large plant, and so on.

add to the attractiveness of charts and diagrams and help make their meaning easier to understand. Such figures are used in Plans 3 and 5.

PAINTINGS AND DIORAMAS

Dioramas are museum displays in which the foreground merges into a colored picture in the background. This gives a feeling of greater distance and more scenery than would otherwise be possible in a museum exhibit. Most people have seen dioramas when they have gone to any fair-sized museum.

It is not likely that the average person will be able to make a diorama by painting the background picture himself. Only somebody with unusual artistic talent can do this. Of course there is the possibility that an artist friend may be willing to help, or that a painting owned by your family may be just what is needed. However, it is possible to provide the picture for a diorama by other means. Large reproductions of good paintings can sometimes be purchased reasonably (through an art store), or even had free if one is part of a large calendar. Such a reproduction of a painting can be glued or pasted in the rear of a display case, and the material in the foreground made to harmonize with the picture by careful arrangement and painting (see Figure 27).

For example, the museum exhibit may be of desert reptiles. You may be able to find a large painting or reproduction of a desert scene that you can use. Paste this with household cement to the rear wall of the glass exhibit case. Then fill in the foreground with a layer of sand and rocks, making it look as much as possible like the sand and rocks in the desert picture. This makes it difficult for the eye of the watcher to tell where the foreground ends and the picture begins. Models of desert plants and lizards are mounted in the foreground in as natural a way as possible (see Chapter 7) so that the scene and the picture behind it seem to merge together. Figure 27 shows the appearance of such a diorama and will give you further ideas on how it is made.

9

Arranging Your Museum Displays for Both Beauty and Storytelling

A Guaymia Indian boy whom I hired to work for me when I was collecting animals in the Panama jungles had seldom worn clothes and had little regard for them. When I took him through the streets of his first big and civilized town, David, the capital of Chiriqui Province, he felt it was much too hot for any kind of covering. So he started to take off his clothes. This caused a near riot plus a great deal of laughter at our expense before I got the clothes back on him.

It is the unusual that draws attention. A giant spider crawling down a wall attracts the eye almost instantly. So does a rattlesnake coiled in a lifelike way, apparently ready to strike. Work for the unusual and the striking in your museum displays to bring them to life before people's eyes. But this is only part of the job in making an interesting and attractive display.

SOME RULES OF ART TO FOLLOW IN MAKING UP MUSEUM DISPLAYS

Museum displays that are arranged without plan, just helter-skelter, are seldom appealing to visitors. On the other hand, some planned displays may not be very attractive simply because the maker didn't understand the rules of art that help displays appeal to the eye.

In each museum display you are telling a story, and your job is to get this story across to a visitor. To do this you have to do the following things:

- Get attention.
- Make the display attractive.
- Show the story told by the display in such a way that even one look will give the visitor a definite feeling of gaining knowledge in a pleasant and interesting way.
- Make the story easy to understand by arranging your printed signs, your specimens, models and so forth in such a way that the eye and mind of your visitor can quickly and easily follow the flow of your story.

How to Get Attention

There are many ways of getting attention. The second paragraph of this chapter describes how to get attention by putting something startling on the wall of your room. There are many other attention getters of this type: a skunk or a porcupine in an attitude of defense, a wildcat about to leap on its prey, a snake swallowing a frog, and so on. Startling pictures in color can be used, as of a great volcano in eruption, or a whale attacked by harpooners, or a giant bear at bay before a pack of dogs.

All your museum displays should have titles. These titles should be printed in very large letters against a background that makes them stand out (see also page 112). Black letters against white is the most common color combination used, but you should experiment with many others. Gold against blue, bright red against green, silver against black—these are good combinations. Some combinations do not work well, such as green against blue, or blue against red. Be sure that your colors do not clash with one another or are not so closely alike that the letters do not stand out as they should.

Each title you print at the head of a display should arouse interest and curiosity. If the title can be tied in closely with an interesting and beautiful picture or with an attractively mounted specimen, then this will often double its value in attracting attention.

Suppose you have a museum display that tells the story of polar exploration, so you put your main title in large black letters: POLAR EXPLORATION. While the subject is interesting enough in itself to attract some attention, you can far more quickly attract the eye and interest of the visitor if you add some punch to the title. For example, put it:

EARTH'S GREATEST ADVENTURE
THE STORY OF POLAR EXPLORATION

Suppose you have a museum display that shows some of the night life on a California desert. So you call it NIGHT LIFE ON A CALIFORNIA DESERT. Interesting? Well, just fairly so, but you can do better. Suppose you print it as SECRETS OF THE DESERT NIGHT. People are interested in secrets. Almost immediately their attention is aroused.

To both of these titles you can add attractive pictures that will give still further help in attracting attention. Suppose, for instance, you put your polar exploration title against a beautiful picture in color of the northern lights with a polar bear killing a seal down below on an ice floe. Immediately the imagination and interest of the visitor are greatly aroused. In the same way you could put your desert night life title in silver letters against a dark and beautiful picture of a desert in the moonlight with the arms of a giant saguaro cactus or a tree yucca standing against the sky.

Titles can attract greater attention according to the way the light strikes them and the way borders or lines are drawn around them. Examples are shown in Plans 2, 3 and 5.

Making your whole display attractive and interesting is, of course, another way to arouse attention. A discussion of this follows.

Making Your Display Attractive

Making your display attractive depends on some of the elementary principles of art. These include balance, structure, emphasis, proportion and movement. *Proportion* is probably the most important of these. You have only so much space for your museum display. Into this space you must put your models, specimens and printed explanations arranged into such attractive shapes and sizes that all will appear as a unified whole. They should be in correct proportion to each other. Plans 2, 3 and 5 show good proportions. Use these examples to help you in planning your proportions. Also get friends who have artistic ability to criticize your layout of a display as shown first in a drawing.

Structure is closely related to proportion, as it deals with the division of space. You soon realize that some shapes are more pleasing when placed together than are others. A lot of squares are monotonous and uninteresting. A lot of circles, rectangles and so forth all thrown in together are equally bad because there is no planned relationship between them. Shapes that too sharply contrast with each other, such as a circle and a rectangle, or a square and a circle, can only be put together in the same display with great care. Ordinarily they will cause a clash to the eye that is not pleasing. If one of the shapes is much smaller than the other, as with the triangles and half-circle in Plan 2, then the contrast is more pleasing and acceptable.

We go back to the Greeks for the great artistic laws of structure, balance and proportion. If you are using different sized rectangles in a museum display, then you use the Greek law of proportion. This states that divisions of space are attractively arranged when the smallest is more than half, and less than two-thirds the size of the next larger. Put into numbers, the sizes appear as 4:7:11, or 3:5:8. The left side of Plan 5 shows the working of this law, for there you see three rectangular pictures with proportionate sizes of about 3:5:8.

The size of the sides of the rectangles you have in your museum displays should follow the golden ratio of the Greeks. This means that the short and long side of each rectangle should have a ratio of about 4 to 7 or 3 to 5. Most books take one of these ratios in their shape. This book, for example, is 6 inches wide by 9 inches long, or a ratio of 2 to 3. Too long a rectangle or too square a rectangle is less pleasing.

Balance depends on the optical center of your display and the grouping of the display material about that center. The optical center is usually slightly above the true or mathematical center. In other words, to the human eye this point appears to be the center, and you should make your material balance on all sides of it.

There are two types of balance. First is formal balance where both sides of an exhibit or series of exhibits are just about equal in shape and arrangement. Formal balance is shown in Plan 3, where the exhibits on both sides of the bookcase are similar in size and shape. Informal balance appears when the exhibits are not distributed equally, yet are so placed as to give a feeling of balance. Plan 5 shows an example of informal balance. In both formal and informal balance, however, all the displays should be in balance around the optical center. The optical center in Plan 3, for example, is about half an inch above the center of the bookcase.

Emphasis is usually handled by arrangement of titles, and is principally gained by contrast. One rule to follow is not to try to emphasize too many things, as then no one of them will be emphasized enough. The printing of titles can be arranged in different sizes, shapes or colors to give emphasis. Different colors are particularly useful in museum displays, as long as the colors harmonize. For instance, you can have your main title in red; then, if two different sets of facts are given in your display, have the printed signs of one set in green and the other in black. This helps emphasize each part of the display and contrast the main ideas shown. Different shapes or sizes of the letters do the same thing.

No more than one or two points of emphasis should be in the same display, as too many take away the attention of the watcher and annoy him or her. To be sure of emphasis in a title it is necessary to use big letters and to have plenty of free and contrasting space around it. If other words are printed near the title or models or specimens mounted too near it, then the title loses much of its attraction-getting value and emphasis. Be sure the contrast in color is pleasing to the eye and clear, such as black against white, gold against blue, red against green, and so forth. Avoid clashing colors or those too closely alike.

Movement gives a feeling of life to a display and also helps attract attention and adds emphasis. Even arrows or lines pointing down to a title give a feeling of movement and draw the eye instantly to the main point of emphasis. The eye follows lines of movement. For example, if the eye sees a wildcat in the act of jumping, the eye follows in the direction of that movement to see what the wildcat is jumping at.

This natural tendency of the eye to follow movement can be of great help to you in placing your emphasis. For example, if you show two mounted animals chasing each other, have the eye follow this movement to a printed sign that describes the animals. It is best to direct movement in a museum display towards the center of the exhibit. If the movement is toward the outside, it will tend to draw the attention away elsewhere.

Neatness, naturalness and *cleanliness* are the final artistic requirements of an attractive museum display. Your lettering of captions and titles should look neat and professional (suggestions as to lettering will be found on page 112). Your mounted specimens and models not only should have a neat appearance, but should look as lifelike as possible. This means careful mounting, molding and coloring. Try to place animals, for instance, in natural positions, as if running or just about to leap, or standing alertly to listen. Lastly, everything about your exhibits should be clean. Nothing so takes away from attractiveness as seeing streaks or smudges of dirt where they should not be.

Show an Attractive Story

To show an attractive story, unity is important. In other words, there should be one main story, not many. If you are going to tell how sedimentary rocks were developed, for example, tell exactly that in as interesting a way as possible. Don't use half of your display to illustrate how sedimentary rocks are used in industry. That is another story needing another museum display. There should be nothing to pull away your visitor's attention from the main idea your display is trying to tell him.

It is also necessary for the visitor to catch right away what the story is about and to see that it is an interesting subject. Pictures, color, diagrams, mounted specimens and models all need to be arranged so that they instantly arouse interest, curiosity and the beginning of understanding. Anything confusing or vague about your museum display will immediately cause the visitor to lose interest and turn away.

On the other hand, increased understanding produces a feeling of delight and accomplishment in the human mind. Your titles and subtitles should clearly lead the visitor on toward this understanding. For example, in a museum display telling the story of sedimentary rocks, you could have titles and subtitles something like these:

A BILLION-YEAR MIRACLE
THE STORY OF SEDIMENTARY ROCKS

Rock made from sea rain	*Rock made from the washed-away wealth of continents*	*Rock made from the death of cliffs*
limestone	shale	breccia
	sandstone	
	conglomerate	

With these titles, three great but connected divisions of your museum display, each with a story to rouse curiosity, become part of the immediate knowledge of your visitor. He is quickly led on into further exploration and discovery, especially if the mounted specimens of this display are attractively chosen and arranged.

Make the Story Easy to Understand

Your story done with diagrams, pictures, specimens, models and printed signs or captions should not only be easy to understand, but it also should look easy to understand. Very few people who look at a museum display are going to take the time to read a long, closely typewritten page explaining it. Captions with comparatively large, easily read print and with few words must do the story. The visitor who looks at your museum exhibit wants to understand the whole story in a matter of seconds, not of minutes.

The parts of your story must be connected in a logical and easily understood way. In other words, the visitor who looks at your display must be able to follow from one caption and one diagram, picture, specimen or model to another without difficulty and with full understanding. One way to help him do this is to number each part of your exhibit, so the onlooker's eye goes easily from 1 to 2 to 3 and so forth. Another way is to use colored ribbons or lines to connect different parts of your display. Still another way is to run a series of arrows from one part of the exhibit to another as the story goes.

Pictures, diagrams, specimens and models should be used as much as possible to take the place of words. Not only are they more interesting to look at, but they are also more easily understood. Also, if mounted specimens or models are so arranged as to tell stories by their action or appearance, they save many words. Showing a beetle grub actually boring a hole through wood, for example, makes it unnecessary to tell how it is done.

HAND LETTERING TITLES AND CAPTIONS

Lettering by hand is easy for some people and difficult for others. Fortunately there are a number of ways to help yourself if you are not by ability a good letter draftsman. If you have only fair ability you can help yourself by drawing two parallel lines on your board or paper. Make them the distance apart that fits the size of the letters you want to make. Then use a ball-point pen or a brush of the proper width for making your letters. Books are listed in Appendix B that will help you further. After you have inked in the letters erase the pencil lines with an art gum eraser.

For people who are very poor at lettering, large stationery stores carry letter stencil sheets of heavy paper in which the forms of the letters are cut through the paper. A brush may then be dipped in ink or paint and painted over the cut letter when it is held above the proper place on your museum display mount. Metal letter forms are also sold by these same stores and may be used for such printing. Both paper and metal forms come with different-sized letters. Sometimes your local grocery or hardware store has a machine for cutting out the letters and will be glad to cut out an alphabet for you. Stationery and art stores also carry sheets of letters backed onto coated paper; by rubbing lightly with a pencil, you can transfer the letters onto another surface to spell out your message.

Another possibility, though a bit more expensive, is to send to Fototype, Inc., 1414 Roscoe St., Chicago, IL 60657, for sets of letters. Ask for their catalogue and prices. These letters may be glued directly to your display, spelling out the words of titles and captions. In all such letter work, household cement is the best pasting medium. Large black letters cut out of magazines and filed away for use alphabetically in small envelopes (preferably transparent) will give you the same thing with less cost but a lot more work.

Paste all such letters between ruled lines on your display mount to make a neat and orderly appearance.

In all lettering and labeling work of this kind practice improves you. Keep trying.

COMPLETING YOUR EXHIBIT

In the earlier pages of this book you have been given all the information you need for completing natural history museum exhibits. But to get a unified picture of how it is done, it seems worthwhile now to review from start to finish the job of making two museum displays for the wall of a room.

The first task is to make a diagram or drawing showing how you want to place your exhibits along the wall. Plan 5 illustrates how this is done, though your plan can be much simpler. There is informal balance in the arrangement of these exhibits. This means the two halves of the wall are not equal in appearance (formal balance), but give a feeling of balance because the amount of material shown on each side is about equal.

Notice that everything is arranged in rectangles of different sizes. Even the circles of the maps and the enlargements of microscopic life are placed inside rectangles. The rectangles are made of different sizes to correspond to the Greek law of proportion, or a ratio of 3:5:7. This gives a pleasing feeling to both displays.

The attention-getting features of the titles are worth observing. Both titles arouse curiosity and interest. The titles are placed against backgrounds that excite further interest and are at the same time very appropriate. The polar-expedition title appears against

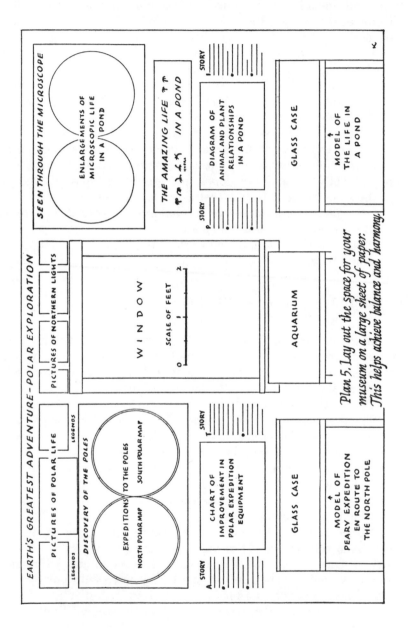

Plan 5. Lay out the space for your museum on a large sheet of paper. This helps achieve balance and harmony.

the shimmering curtains of the northern lights, painted in vivid colors. The pond-life title appears in a setting of actual cattails, preserved under a coating of transparent plastic.

Making the Polar-Exploration Exhibit

The polar-exploration exhibit shown in Plan 5 is an example of what can be done with a museum display when you have no actual specimens. Of course most of the specimens of tools, writings and so on of the great polar expeditions are both very rare and very valuable, and so are in large public museums. But the private person has little chance of obtaining any of these. To make the display described here it is necessary to use pictures, maps, diagrams and models to take the place of specimens. Yet see what a fine display and an interesting story can be shown.

NOTE: Sometimes, by special permission, a museum will let you make a plaster or rubber mold of a specimen they have.

The pictures used in this exhibit are selected from magazines like *National Geographic, Nature,* or *Natural History.* Those pictures that are not colored are hand-painted with watercolors to make them more attractive, and all are placed as shown in Plan 5.

Maps of the polar regions can be found in old *National Geographic* magazines, taken from an old atlas or bought by ordering them at some bookstores or special map stores. It may be necessary to do research at your local library to find the routes of exploration taken by each of the great polar explorers. These routes should be marked on the maps with different-colored inks or pencils. This should be done very clearly so each route is plain to see.

The chart of improvement in polar-expedition equipment is another project needing some research. As civilized men kept trying to reach the poles, they had to learn how to live and travel under very difficult conditions. At first they made bad mistakes and their equipment was very primitive. Gradually it improved and they kept getting nearer and nearer the poles. You can easily show this on your chart by giving on the left the dates and names of famous expeditions. Then in columns on the right show by small pictures (drawn or taken from magazines) 1) the kinds of ships the explorers used; 2) the methods they used for breaking through the ice; 3) the kind of camping equipment they used; 4) the kind of food they carried; 5) the kind of sled gear they had; 6) the types of guns and other hunting equipment they used; 7) the kind of clothing they wore, 8) their method of transport, whether animal or mechanical; and 9) miscellaneous information about the expedition.

On either side of the chart tell a brief story of polar expeditions. Give the reasons why men tried to reach the poles, and describe some of the heartbreaks, tragedies and heroism that led up to final victory. Contrast the terrible struggles of the past with the ease of flying to the poles now. This story should be printed plainly on large cards on either side of the chart.

The model of the Peary Expedition (or any other polar expedition) on its way to the North Pole is the hardest part of this exhibit. The glass case should be made as described in Chapter 2 and mounted on wooden legs. In books about the Peary Expedition or in old *National Geographics* of 1909 and 1910 you can find descriptions and pictures of the expedition. These should be studied carefully to help you decide what you are going to include in your model scene.

A typical scene would probably show the expedition about ready to leave its camp on the polar ice pack. To make this a diorama, a large colored picture of an arctic scene would be glued to the back of the museum case (see Chapter 8). The foreground would be made to appear to merge gradually into this picture by carefully using the same colors and general features. A sheet of glass covered with the snow compound used to powder Christmas trees gives a realistic appearance of snow and ice. A pressure ridge, such as appears in the polar ice, may be shown by irregular blocks of plastic or wood piled in a line and covered with the snow material.

In the foreground appears a skin tent and an igloo of snow of the kinds used by Peary's expedition on its dash to the Pole. The igloo should be made of cubes of sugar cut to fit and glued together. The tent may easily be made of sheets of heavy paper painted skin color. In front of the tent are two sleds, one leaving and one waiting to load the tent. The sleds should be made of a light wood painted the color of bone and lashed together with tiny strips of rawhide cut from leather shoelaces with a razor. These sleds are models of the kind of sled Peary used. Each sled is drawn by a team of Husky dogs. The dogs should be rubber models of the small metal or glass dogs often sold in art stores (made as described in Chapter 7). Each has been painted to look like a Husky and harnessed to the sled with small strips of rawhide.

The two men who are with each sled are resin–wax or rubber models of small 6-inch-high metal men (also found at art stores or five-and-ten stores). Each man holds a gun and is dressed in what appears to be Eskimo skin clothing. This may be made of dark brown painted cloth fringed with a little real fur around the head. The real fur can be had from small scraps given away free at almost any fur store or taken from the edge of a rabbit skin. Two of the men and the dogs are running with one sled. The other sled is standing still, being loaded.

The model thus shows in interesting detail the type of equipment used by polar explorers and how they carry it. Naturally many variations can be made in the way the model is arranged, according to the story you want to tell.

Making the Pond-Life Exhibit

The pond-life exhibit shown in Plan 5 can teach a very valuable and exciting lesson. So many millions of people pass by a small pond and have no idea of the way life swarms through every drop of that water. They are strangers to the fantastic insects and worms that hunt through the green depths. They know nothing even about how frogs, snakes and turtles get their food and live in that world within a world, a small pond.

So your title is one to catch and arouse interest. THE AMAZING LIFE IN A POND printed in large bright green letters against a background of brown cattails instantly draws and attracts the eyes. Use color in other parts of your display to attract and draw attention. SEEN THROUGH THE MICROSCOPE, for instance, could be printed in bright red against a green background.

At the top of this exhibit appears a large rectangular sheet of paper with two circles drawn upon it. Inside these circles you show enlargements of microscopic animals and plants that are found in pond water. There are three ways to make these enlargements. One is by drawing them yourself from what you see as you gaze through a microscope. Another way, if you have no artistic ability yourself, is to have a friend draw them who does good artwork. A third way is to find photographs and drawings in magazines such as *Nature* or *Natural History* and place these inside your circles. In all cases, if you can color the animals and plants shown as nearly as possible as they are in life, you will add to the beauty of your exhibit. Each animal and plant should be labeled with its common as well as scientific name (see Chapter 4).

The chart of animal and plant relationships in a pond is much easier to make than it sounds. All you are trying to do is show what the animals and plants have to do with each other. Remember that the plants not only furnish food to many animals, but also many of them give shelter and hiding places. Books on ecology or pond life, such as those listed in Appendix B under "Ecology," usually have diagrams or other information showing which animals in a pond are eaten by which others. Use these diagrams to help you make your chart. A line with an arrow on the end of it pointing from a frog to a fly means that the frog eats the fly. All these arrows combined make what scientists call the "food web" of the pond. A simplified food web is shown in Figure 28.

A big improvement can be had by drawing colored lines between the different animals and plants. The colored lines would help show food chains inside the food web. For example, a tadpole eats green algae in the pond. This would be shown by a red line to illustrate the first part of a food chain. A giant water bug eats the tadpole. This is shown by a green line, to illustrate the second step in the food chain. A bass eats the giant water bug. This is shown by an orange line, making clear the third step. A fisherman catches the bass. A blue line shows this fourth and last step in that particular food chain.

On either side of the chart you place rectangular sheets of heavy paper or cardboard on which you print in easily read letters the story of the amazing life in a pond. Before lettering this, read a good book on freshwater life, such as those listed under "Ecology" in Appendix

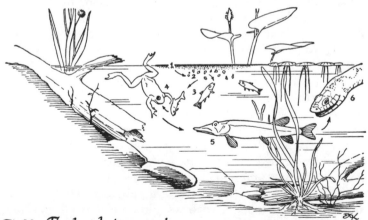

Fig. 28. Food web in a pond.
Algae (1) are eaten by tiny crustaceans (2), which are eaten by small fish (3), which are eaten by frogs (4), which are eaten (along with small fish) by pickerel (5), which are eaten (along with frogs) by water snake (6). Animals not drawn to scale.

B. Also do some careful observing of a pond near your home. Then print a brief, interesting description of what you know about pond life.

The model of life in a pond is put in a glass case (such as is described in Chapter 2). You make the bottom, sides and shores of the pond out of papier-mâché (see page 96). When this material sets and hardens paint it brown as if it were mud. For the surface of the pond you need a sheet of transparent plastic (bought through a hardware or stationery store). Cut this sheet with strong scissors so as to fit the shore of your pond. Cement it into place, leaving the front part of the pond open as if cut in cross section (see Plan 5). Into this opening and around the shores of the pond go your specimens and models.

You are going to show in your model pond some of the animals and plants typical of your neighborhood. So you visit such a pond near your home, studying its appearance and watching carefully for the typical places where each kind of animal and plant is found. Much of what you observe you should write down in your notebook, along with diagrams that help show where things are found. Next you should bring back specimens with you from the pond.

From the plants make resin–wax models or other types of models as explained in Chapter 7. The stems of the shore plants are stuck into holes bored in the papier-mâché of the shore. The stems of the pond plants are stuck down through holes bored in the transparent plastic surface of the pond to other holes drilled in the papier-mâché bottom. Or they are arranged in whatever way is natural to them in the real pond.

Some animal specimens, such as adult water insects, can be mounted with glue or cement to the plastic water surface or to the stems of water plants, spreading the legs in a natural manner. They should then be sprayed with transparent plastic to protect them from pests. To show an insect swimming under water, you have to hold it in place with tiny, nearly invisible wires or threads attached to the plastic and the papier-mâché with cement.

Make the large animals, such as frogs, fish and crayfish, of rubber molding material as described in Chapter 7. When they are made, paint them in their natural colors. Then arrange each in a natural position in or about the pond. A snake, for example, may be shown sneaking up on a frog that is seated on a lily pad. Another snake may be shown eating a frog. A crayfish crawls along the bottom. A fish appears to swim in the middle of the pool (actually, it is hung by almost invisible wires from the plastic surface).

A water spider can be shown carrying its bubble of air down the stem of a water plant. To make the spider model, put a rubber mold around the original spider and then make a resin–wax cast from this. Such a model must be handled very carefully.

A little glue may generally be used to mount specimens realistically on the stones, banks and surface of the pond. Dragonflies and damsel flies can be shown lighting on the leaves of the water plants. Tiger beetles can be placed on the shores, and dragonfly larvae or water tigers shown lurking among the stems of the water plants. A giant water bug can be shown on the bottom attacking a tadpole.

Some of the soft-bodied creatures, like flatworms and leeches, can best be made by hand modeling either from clay or from a soft warm resin–wax mixture. The latter must be molded into shape before it sets. Other soft-bodied animals can be made by the rubber or resin–wax molding method described in Chapter 7.

You can start this exhibit with just a few of the very common animals and plants and gradually add to it. It is a big but very interesting job. It could also be done by a nature club or a class in high school.

The last part of the pond-life exhibit is the aquarium. In the aquarium are placed as many of the animals and plants found in the natural pond as possible. However, be careful not to overcrowd your aquarium, as then most of the animals will die. It is usually necessary to divide your aquarium into two sections with a wire screen or a sheet of glass. Carnivorous animals like the water beetles and water bugs are placed on one side of the screen. Plant-eating animals and scavengers, such as polliwogs, are put on the other side. Otherwise soon all the plant-eating animals would be eaten up by the hunting animals. How to build and maintain an aquarium properly is described in any good book on the subject, obtainable at your library or at a pet or aquarium store.

10

Trading Museum Mounts and Specimens

Trading is one of the most profitable of all ways to enlarge and improve your collections and your museum. There are many things in your neighborhood that you may get very easily but that people in other parts of the world think of as quite valuable. The famous scientist Dr. Raymond L. Ditmars started his career when he was a boy by trading the snakes of New York for those in other states and countries. By careful trading he obtained such beautiful and unusual specimens as the South American bushmaster, coral snakes, Indian python, king cobra and so forth.

It is possible to trade not only actual specimens, living or preserved, but also museum mounts and models. For example, suppose you have made a plaster mold of a local turtle, such as the Pacific pond turtle (*Clemys marmorata*) if you live on the Pacific Coast. You made a rubber model of this turtle and used it in one of your museum displays. But now you have a letter from a man in Virginia who is making a museum display of the turtles of the United States. He is anxious to get a rubber model of the Pacific pond turtle. You ask him what he has to trade, and maybe he has a copy of *National Geographic* that you would like to have because of the pictures of animals in it. Or maybe he has a rubber model of a certain lizard you would like to have. So you make up a copy of the Pacific pond turtle and the two of you trade. Both of you get valuable additions to your museums.

Collectors who are willing to trade can be found all over the world. Below is an address to which you can write for information about lists of naturalists and collectors:

The Naturalist's Directory, 43rd Edition, 1978. World Natural History Publications, P.O. Box 550, Marlton, New Jersey 08053.

Naturalist's Directory (International), 42nd Edition, 1975. World Natural History Publications (address as above).

These two books will help you contact naturalists in different parts of the world who may have specimens, models or photographs that would be helpful to have in your museum. The books are re-published about every five years; you may get your own name and address placed in them.

Another book that lists scientists and naturalists of all types and their addresses is *Who Knows—and What,* published by the A. N. Marquis Company, Chicago, Illinois. Most libraries have a copy of this book in their reference section.

Look through these lists and books and try to find the names of people who have interests similar to yours and who you think might have something to trade in which you would be interested. Write each one a courteous letter asking if he or she would be interested in trading, or knows somebody who would, and telling what you have to exchange. A self-addressed, stamped return envelope or a post-card put in with your letter is a mark of courtesy that will help en-sure an answer.

It is foolish to send poorly packed specimens or models to peo-ple with whom you are trading. If what you send arrives damaged, you will have to replace it or lose a friend and trader.

Both specimens and models should be packed in wooden or metal boxes that are strong enough to take a lot of rough handling in the mails. Cotton, sawdust or crumpled paper should be firmly packed around the contents for protection. If you use a cigar box, the roof must be reinforced with nailed-in strips of wood. (See also page 42 for instructions on mailing and packaging.) Always replace lost or broken material promptly. Valuable specimens or models should al-ways be sent insured.

The smart museum maker will soon find many with whom he can make good trades. But perhaps most of all, he will find many fine friendships all over the earth and will steadily add to his own knowl-edge through these contacts with others. Good luck and good trad-ing!

11

Other Ideas and Improvements for Exhibits

SUGGESTED INNOVATIVE EXHIBITS

These suggestions are made to stretch you imagination, to help you see beyond the commonplace and create something that is unique and that will greatly expand the minds of your friends and others—and perhaps even help to make a better world. Your exhibits can be part of the vital fight for a better environment for us all and for better human relations as well.

As you begin to develop any of these ideas, or ideas you make up yourself, try to think of each project as a scientist would. The scientist looks at a subject or project from every possible angle and carefully experiments and investigates as much as is possible. The scientist tries to discover the truth and to reveal it without allowing prejudices or selfish ideas to interfere. This way he or she may create new ideas or make wonderful discoveries of value to all humanity. Here are some suggestions.

1. Show how the kinds of homes used by American Indians in the old days depended on the kind of country they lived in. Papier-mâché or modeling clay may be used to shape the hills of New England, for example; artificial trees made of sticks and papier-mâché may show the forest; while other materials may be used to make a walled village showing how the Indians protected themselves against enemies. A typical bark-and-stick house of that time and place can demonstrate, inside and out, with weapons and tools in evidence, how the people lived. Show the clothes worn, the bark dishes made for eating, pottery if it was also made, and

123

whatever was suitable for that environment and special culture.

In time, you could make similar village scenes and homes for such tribes as the Sioux in their tepees, the Mandans in their log and mud houses, and the Pueblo peoples in adobe towns with high, windowless walls for defense. The main thrust of your work and creativity would be to make each home and each scene of village life as authentic as possible.

2. Show how increased water pressure and darkness change the life of the sea as you go deeper beneath the waves. Make plastic waves above with white-painted crests; plastic sheets stretching below might catch the shimmer from a hidden light that would act as sunlight would. You could paint on the plastic the bodies of various sea creatures. Or you could take pictures out of magazines such as *National Geographic* and paste them on the plastic to show whales, seals, sharks and other fish going about their business in the sea. Luminescent lights might be down below in the darkest places.

3. Show and compare the homes and towns made by different kinds of ants, bees and wasps—the social insects—pointing out how each adapts to its surroundings and how each defends against enemies. Termites could be added to this scene as another social insect. The homes could be molded out of papier-mâché or clay, adapted from pictures in magazines such as *National Geographic* and *Natural History,* and made as natural-looking as possible. Insect societies are fascinating when understood, and it should be your earnest desire and work to demonstrate to as many people as possible, in a clear and understandable way, how these creatures construct and use their homes and towns.

4. When something destructive and dangerous is happening to a part of the earth, we have a great need to show it in a fine museum exhibit. Often an excellent, well-illustrated magazine article shows what is happening, but a magazine is too often put aside and forgotten. We can continue to emphasize the problem and the great need for overcoming it by doing a top-notch museum exhibit on the subject, which could be even more interesting and dramatic than the article. A really well-done project might be duplicated in other places.

For example, in the August 1983 issue of *National Geo-*

graphic there is a fine article on "The Mississippi's Disappearing Delta." The article shows in detail how many of the activities of humans in this area of the delta are destructive and how the delta is being rapidly destroyed. Maps and diagrams, plus fine color photographs, could demonstrate how this is happening. But this is shown, of course, only on a small scale in the magazine. Enlarging everything shown, say, six to ten times, would bring home clearly and forcefully the difficulties and the wrong decisions that have hurt the delta.

5. Form a museum club and keep building it until you can not only have a yearly exhibit in a hall of interesting projects developed in your area, but can also invite museum exhibit makers from other cities and towns to bring their offerings. At such gatherings, exhibits, models, photographs and other objects can be traded or learned from.

6. Get fellow museum makers in other cities and towns with whom you have been corresponding to send you photographs or drawings of their exhibits and send your own photos and drawings to them, so that all can learn and improve on their exhibits. Keep an album of these and study them for ideas you can use.

7. Always be on the lookout for ways to improve an exhibit you have made. Lighting effects are always a good way to do this. For example, a hidden light shining through colored screens or plastic sheets may beautifully tint the objects in your exhibit, emphasizing what you want the exhibit to say. Sometimes just changing the direction of the light can greatly enhance your exhibit.

8. When you can afford a small electric motor, you can introduce motion into a museum exhibit and catch the attention of watchers in startling or enlightening ways. Little belts that move behind the scenes can bring moving people and animals across the stage. For example, you can show wolves hunting an elk, or Eskimo hunters hunting a polar bear.

9. Running water offers a way to make an exhibit more realistic. You can "create" a running creek with the kind of water life found in creeks, or you can make a waterfall and show the nest of a water ouzel behind the fall with the tiny baby birds (done as models) opening their mouths to take worms from an adult. If you have real insects and their larvae in the creek, you would stop these creatures from escaping by

placing a screen across the lower end of the creek. Think of many other ways in which you can do interesting things with water.

10. A hand crank can be used along with pulleys and threads or small ropes to create movement. A screen can also be made that turns on a hand crank and tells a story about your exhibit by pictures and words. If the watcher is able to turn the crank to see what will happen, this makes it even more interesting to him or her. Such a screen would move between two rollers and so could be rolled back to put into position for a new showing. Make your printing quite plain and easy to read, and make your pictures colorful and as animated as possible.

SCIENTIFIC EXHIBITS

There are many ways to create—and then to regard—scientific exhibits and projects, far more than I have room to tell about in this book. Use your imagination and build on what is suggested here.

Science, or the scientific method, should be considered a means of exploring all phases of existence to try to understand and use it intelligently. But it is a job that has to be done carefully, diligently and in a well-balanced way to be truly scientific. For example, take a flashlight that does not work. Without investigation, it would be foolish to insist that the only problem is the batteries. As a scientist, you would have an open mind to every possible reason why the flashlight is not working and test each one with equal care. You use what is called "the theory of multiple working hypotheses."

For example, you consider the following hypotheses about a nonworking flashlight: 1) it needs new batteries; 2) it needs a new globe; 3) the adjustments of the working parts are not right, so no electricity is getting to the light; 4) somewhere corrosion is causing loss of electricity. After writing down these four hypotheses and any others you can think of, you then carefully test each one until you find the one or more causing the trouble, and "presto" the flashlight is fixed! This is the scientific attitude and method.

Of course, in science there are many more complicated and difficult problems than this one. Exhibits to show how problems in science have been solved in the past, or how they might be solved in the future, can be very instructive of how fine minds work and can encourage others to use their minds for similar discoveries. The follow-

ing sections discuss some possible scientific exhibits of varying difficulty.

The Discovery of Planets

Uranus, Neptune and Pluto are planets that cannot be seen at
night with unaided eyes.* It takes binoculars to see Uranus and
Neptune, and a powerful telescope to see distant Pluto. You could
make an exhibit that would show how these three planets were discovered by astronomers, incorporating photographs of the actual instruments used, of the planets after they were discovered, and of the
solar system as a whole. You could try to explore how scientists
could tell where the new planets were in the sky by their effect on
other planets, particularly Jupiter and Saturn. You could also tell
and illustrate in your exhibit how a still more remote planet might
yet be discovered.

Other Discoveries in Astronomy

Astronomers are divided into two kinds, professionals and amateurs. Professionals handle the huge telescopes and other highly
complicated and costly machines that are generally used only on the
more sophisticated and difficult problems of astronomy. But amateur astronomers, with much less costly telescopes, can do valuable
work, especially if they have the patience to view small sections of
the sky that the big telescopes do not have time for, and watch pa-
tiently, night after night, over a long period of time for new objects
or phenomena to come into view. In this way, many amateur astronomers have discovered asteroids, binary and variable stars, and
comets. See if you can demonstrate effectively how an amateur
makes such a vital discovery; try to convey some of the excitement
involved in making these discoveries.

Researching Other Topics

You can find interesting topics for exhibits by exploring a library and obtaining the help of the assistant librarians who delve
into specialized materials. The *Subject Guide to Books in Print*

---

* If you live in an area with no light pollution, Uranus is just visible to
the naked eye. The presence of city lights, however, makes it impossible to
see unaided.

(found in all libraries and most bookstores), for example, can help you find almost any book you need. And there are large books that record all the articles published in different magazines, by title and by subject. Ask your reference librarian to show you these.

For example, you might like to find out more about the prehistoric-type culture—the Tassaday—recently discovered in the jungles of Mindanao, the large southern island of the Philippines. This is a fascinating story, since when the Tassaday were found, they were almost completely cut off from modern civilization. Isolated in thick jungle, they use the ancient ways of living known by our ancestors perhaps ten thousand years ago. You would look up and study all books, articles and scientific papers about the Tassaday, using your library as your main resource. Then you would build an exhibit of photographs, drawings, diagrams and models that would show in detail how the Tassaday live and what they do socially, spiritually, physically and culturally. You could explain how the Tassaday were discovered, and show adventures of how they hunt game or gather other types of foods. If you could obtain a record or tape of the sounds made at their dances and ceremonies, you could really make your story of this people come alive. In all such attempts to bring home to an audience the true drama and life of a people or other living creatures and plants, you need to develop an intimate investigation of their lives by the scientific method, trying to uncover every significant detail.

Animal Ecology

The science of ecology opens up many and varied explorations into the interactions and effects upon each other and the earth of different plants, animals and humankind. Investigations into these subjects can then be beautifully and dramatically put into a museum display that makes the subject far clearer and more interesting to most people than just talking about it.

For example, many ranchers, especially sheepmen and, to a lesser extent, cattlemen, consider that all mountain lions and coyotes are totally their enemies and should be destroyed. They call on the government to foster extensive campaigns to eradicate them. If you investigated this subject as a scientist would, you would soon find many fascinating trails traveled by others before you; and you would gradually begin to put together a picture of the whole subject that would likely be nearer the truth than the prejudiced view of many ranchers.

You would find, for example, that ecologists have discovered that mountain lions are often essential to the life of forests and that their value in this direction might far offset the harm they do to livestock. For example, when almost all lions were killed off in the Kaibab Forest in northern Arizona, the deer herd increased enormously from about 3,000 individuals to around 30,000, so that many young trees were stripped of their bark and died because of the ravenous deer that were no longer kept under control by the mountain lions.

Mountain lions have other value to us. To see a lion in the wilderness, as I have several times, is to experience the tremendous thrill of discovering a wonderfully interesting creature. Think of and discover for yourself things to value about this animal, and demonstrate them through pictures, maps, models and other media.

The coyote is hated by ranchers far more than the lion is, especially by shepherds when they find their sheep killed or wounded by coyotes. Biologists point out, however, that only certain coyotes become sheep killers and the bulk of coyotes are a valuable part of the balance of life in woods and prairies. Often the bloody work of wild dogs is blamed on coyotes.

Coyotes efficiently limit populations of rodents and rabbits, which would otherwise destroy vast quantities of grasses and other valuable forage crops. If they are wiped out, as sheepmen almost universally desire, might not the loss of forage food for the sheep produce more deaths by starvation than the coyote could do by killing, especially if the sheep were well guarded? Your answer to this question could be magnificently presented through dramatic pictures, diagrams and other ways of illustrating and making clear the facts.

Another facet of this problem to explore is the use of guard dogs trained to guard sheep from coyotes and other predators. These dogs (find out about them with the help of your reference librarian!) are raised with the sheep as puppies and so trained and habit-formed as to become effective and ferocious defenders of the sheep when they grow up. Some sheep ranchers, once badly bothered by coyotes and wild dogs who killed their sheep, found the guard dogs so effective in driving the coyotes and outlaw pet dogs away that all such sheep-killing on their ranches was completely ended! You could dramatically illustrate facts like these and thus make the whole problem of sheep and coyotes become much more interesting to your viewers. If you could ever get a recording on tape of a battle between sheep dogs and coyotes in the night, what a glorious proof of hero dogs that would be! What I have given here is probably only a small part of what a real scientific investigation of this subject would uncover.

Plant Ecology

Plant ecology is a world in itself, almost as wide as animal ecology. And, of course, another vast field to explore and exhibit in your museum lies in the interaction between plants and animals. Let's first, however, consider here a plainly made plant ecology exhibit, one of a myriad that could be done in a scientific manner. As in all scientific work, what you want to do is find out, explain and demonstrate with dramatic pictures, models and so forth the true picture of the subject you choose. Truthfulness in science is vital—it is the only way to have a valid effect on your viewers.

Some eighty years ago, for example, a man who considered himself a scientist and explorer, and was even considered so at that time by many other people, tried with an elaborate display of seeming facts to prove that he had been the first human being to reach the North Pole. For a while, some important people and organizations actually believed him and newspapers hailed him as a hero. But close investigations of his records soon showed that he was telling a lie, and his name, which once seemed to loom big in history, faded into obscurity. It would be interesting to find out who this man was and make a museum demonstration of what he did and of all the ramifications of his hoax.

But here let us consider in more detail an interesting project in plant ecology and a museum display that would make it come alive. You do not have to live in desert country to make a good display of desert plants. You can create a small artificial desert with a sun lamp, and with young plants of cactus, mesquite, acacia and creosote bush, bought at nominal expense. These plants need little water and rather sandy soil. You want to show why and how these plants are successful in a harsh environment. So your artificial desert garden should duplicate desert conditions as closely as possible, which means long periods without water and then sudden drenchings, as happens during a thundershower. You would keep records of how the plants grow, protect themselves and interact together, noticing how a dog or cat or different kinds of birds treat them. The creosote bush is a fierce competitor. The creosote-like smell it gives off and the oils it drips into the ground may cause other plants to shy away from it, giving it room in which to grow and find nourishment. See if this is true by trying to grow other plants in the soil next to a creosote bush. What happens to these plants? Tell the story in a chart with pictures.

The jumping cholla cactus is a competitor in a different way. It is especially combative toward animals and human beings. It does not want them to come too near and its spiny joints seem to actually jump at you if you come too close to the cactus. Once those spines have stuck to you, they may be hard to pull off, especially if you use fingers. The best way to get them off is with a pair of pliers or a long pair of tweezers. Imagine a poor animal, like a coyote, getting one of those things stuck to its nose! Trying to get the horrid thing off with a paw or by rubbing might make conditions worse. A young and inexperienced animal soon learns a big lesson: Never, no never, get near a cholla cactus!

The barrel cactus has spines to protect itself, too, covering every inch of its barrel-like body. But what is the barrel for? It has accordion-like folds inside with many air ducts and chambers, which can be filled with water when a good rain comes. Thus, it is a storer of life-giving water, though you cannot actually drink from it even when you cut it open. The knowledgeable American Indians would cut it with a knife, then take the pieces and pound them in a stone bowl until the water flowed out in droplets they eagerly soaked their food in. What a vital way to stay alive in 100° F (43° C) heat!

The mesquite bush has many finely divided little leaves and also branchlets with numerous sharp thorns. The leaves are tiny so that they do not lose too much moisture to the air, but the mesquite has another way besides rain to get moisture for its living cells. Down below it has very long roots that must almost literally dig and squirm down through the earth until they reach water, even as far as 35 feet below the surface! Such plants are generally found on the edges of dry streambeds, where those deep-searching roots can find the hidden water they want. How do these plants do without water in your garden? Everything each plant does to stay alive should be told in charts, pictures and stories.

You also can use pictures, charts and models to illustrate the different stages of growth of your desert plants. Be sure that in the springtime you give the plants enough water to let them bloom. In the true desert, if water is unavailable for a long time, plants refuse to bloom because to try would only be a waste of energy and help kill them. But when water comes, often the flowering is like an explosion, so eager are the plants to open their flowers while water is available. Be sure to time exactly how long each flower takes to grow. See if you can notice the difference in one twenty-four-hour period after a rain (which can be artificial) in your garden. Of course, to flower the plants need not only rain, but the correct amount of sunlight and heat.

You also can make a diorama (for example, a painting) to show desert life. If you are not an expert artist, you can still make a wall diorama, using pictures from magazines, or even by blowing up pictures of plants and animals from pictures in books and magazines (see next section).

Ecological Displays

Let us prepare a diorama of a streamside woodland in western Iowa, the very center of North America, and show some of the relations between plants and animals in this habitat. Since you are not a very good artist, you decide to do the whole diorama by making everything by enlargements from pictures or diagrams in books and magazines. Suppose you make your diorama 7 feet long and 4 feet high. With a light pencil (which can be easily erased) draw squares on the diorama, each 4 by 4 inches in size. From studying ecology and botany books about Iowa, you determine the common plants in this kind of habitat. When you know what plants you are going to use, draw the rough outline of a little creek wandering down through the lower part of the picture, using a light pencil, yet marking strongly enough that it is clearly visible. The water for this creek can be made of green plastic cut to fit the creek lines you have drawn. Rocks can be made to stick out of the middle, where you will later put frogs and other water creatures.

Different trees that grow along a stream in that part of Iowa can be found in books or magazines and then enlarged by drawing squares—perhaps 1 inch by 1 inch—over these pictures. You then expand what is in a 1-by-1-inch square as part of a tree and make it fit onto the larger 4-by-4-inch square of the diorama. This actually makes a tree on the diorama appear eight times as big as the original. It can then be colored and filled in to look as much as possible like the full-color tree painting or photograph in the magazine or book. When you put other plants in and also birds, mammals, snakes and so forth, remember that you are not limited to exactly the same enlargements for each one but can handle each as you enlarge it so it fits most naturally into the diorama.

When you have a complete diorama, with many plants and animals looking as natural as possible, you can take a transparent sheet of plastic as large as the diorama with sticky transparent tape to hold it, and then mark on the plastic the names of the animal and plant species, plus lines that indicate such things as which animals eat which plants or other animals, which plants are saprophytes or parasites, which are vines and so forth. After a group of people or a class from school has looked at this named display of plant and animal species and studied the lines that tell who eats whom, you could take the whole plastic oversheet down and ask the group that came to write down the names and see how correct they are about which animals are meat eaters and which plant eaters. To make this somewhat easier, every plant and animal could be numbered so that your visitors could try to put the correct name after a number.

Plastic oversheets with other information, such as types of soil different plants like, or the habits of different animals and birds, could be put on the new oversheet and again used for testing or for games. A whole show of this sort could be done with a smaller number of species, bringing out their relationships in depth and showing how the scientific method increased knowledge. Use your imagination and design these new ideas on different dioramas.

Science Projects with Rocks, Minerals and Fossils

Rocks. Rocks are of three major kinds: 1) igneous, caused by the cooling into solid rocks of hot molten rock rising up under the earth's skin; 2) sedimentary, caused by the transformation under pressure of sedimentlike mud into shale, or sand into sandstone, or small rocks cemented into conglomerate; 3) metamorphic, caused by the transformation through great heat and pressure of rocks such as marble, slate, schist and gneiss into semicrystalline hard rocks. You can take any one of these rocks—marble, for example—and test it in every possible way for hardness (with a knife or piece of quartz or a penny), colors, reaction to hydrochloric acid (marble fizzes along a crack or scratch), and so forth. On a board covered with paper, you can make a display of how the rock reacted to every test, with drawings and actual parts of the rock. Comparisons can then be made with other rocks put to the same tests. If any rocks lend themselves to particular uses (soapstone, for example, can be used for simple carving), these uses can be put on your display board to increase knowledge of rocks.

Minerals. Actual scientific tests can be done with rocks, but first you have to learn their mineral content. A mineral is different from a rock, which is usually made up of two or more different minerals. Each mineral is a unit that cannot be separated into different parts, but is cohesive. You can explore minerals by testing their hardness, investigating their crystalline structure and noting their reaction to heat or acids. You can then speculate on how these qualities make the minerals useful.

You can also make all kinds of fancy and interesting exhibits of minerals, for example: 1) show all the colors and uses of quartz minerals; 2) show the many kinds of mineral hardnesses and how each can be used; 3) make your own mineral crystals by the proper use of heat and water and show in a display how this can be done; 4) make a crystal display of all the kinds of mineral crystals and explain how each is used in jewelry, industry and so on; 5) show how a mineral is designed and used for specific work in industry, and possibly imagine and describe ways minerals might be used that would be new advances in mineralogy. (This last suggested project would need a great deal of research through the help of your librarian and probably a visit with an experienced mineralogist to get ideas. It could be your major project and display because it would require a great deal of work.)

Fossils. Fossils are a special world, and I encourage you to read books on fossils, such as those listed in Appendix B at the back of this book. From such reading you can put together such scientific projects as the following:

1. Construct a fossil diorama of the fossils found in your neighborhood, using both pictures and actual specimens when available, showing complete records, if possible, of their locations, the rock strata involved, their kinds and their place in earth history.
2. Take one interesting fossil and trace its history as much as it is known and its relationship to the other fossils of the same period, finding out everything you can about it. Doing much research at the library, plus obtaining actual specimens in the field, would make this a major project and display. I once did this with a project on the history and nature of the belemnites, large bullet-shaped fossils of animals that were related to the squids but had long, pointed bullet-like shells for protection. I found myriads of the shells in some crumbly, dark, clayish soil in the hills of northeastern Wyoming. I showed in my display how the belemnites had derived from

more primitive types of crustaceans and also tried to show how they probably died off because new and large sharks were able to break into their shells. It was a fascinating project! This close examination of one specific fossil can be scientific work of great value. I don't expect you to make a great discovery, but if you do it right, you will be working like a research scientist.

CONCLUSION

These stories of how to make exhibits and the diagrams that go with them are only suggestions and aids to start you on your way. In the wide range of the world and the universe there must be many millions of subjects that could be put into fascinating exhibits. From any of the books listed in Appendix B you can draw ideas for exhibits of your own. You will discover that good museum makers and curators are among the happiest of all human beings. Their hands and their brains are active in so many interesting ways that every hour of living seems full of adventure. I can wish you no better luck than to be one of this group, one of the makers of the museums of tomorrow.

Appendix A

Topics to Investigate
in Museum Projects

Look up books and magazines in your library that provide information on these subjects.

ANTHROPOLOGY

Caucasian–American Indian
  relations
Physical Anthropology
Social Anthropology
Tribes of America
Tribes of other lands

ASTRONOMY

Comets
Exploring the universe
Meteors and meteorites
Moons
Nebulae
Planetoids
Planets
Star clusters
Star types
Strange objects and forces
  in space
The Sun

BIOLOGY

Interactions of plants and
  animals

BOTANY

Algae
Angiosperms
Bacteriology
Ferns
Gymnosperms
Mosses and liverworts
Mycology
Plant Ecology
Plant Pathology
Plant Physiology

CLIMATOLOGY

Amateur weather forecasting
Meteorology

Storms and effects
Study of clouds
Sun, effects of
Water, effects of

GEOLOGY

Geomorphology
Mineralogy

MANKIND AND
THE EARTH

Balance with nature
Imbalance with nature
Science and peace
Science and understanding
Science versus prejudice

PALEONTOLOGY

Invertebrate Paleontology
Vertebrate Paleontology

PETROLOGY

Crystallography
Earthquakes
Glaciation
Magnetism
Mines
Tectonic Plates
Vulcanism

ZOOLOGY

Anatomy
Animal Ecology
Embryology
Entomology
Ethology
Herpetology
Invertebrates
Mammalogy
Microbiology
Ornithology
Pathology
Physiology
Social insects

Appendix B

Books to Read

NATURE STUDY AND NATURAL HISTORY

Beller, Joel. *So You Want to Do a Science Project!* Arco, 1982.
Borland, Hal. *The Golden Circle: A Book of Months.* Harper & Row, 1977.
Brown, Vinson. *The Amateur Naturalist's Diary.* Prentice-Hall, 1982.
———. *The Amateur Naturalist's Handbook.* Prentice-Hall, 1980.
———. *Investigating Nature Through Outdoor Projects.* Stackpole, 1983.
———. *Reading the Outdoors at Night.* Stackpole, 1972.
Carson, Rachel. *The Sense of Wonder.* Harper & Row, 1965.
Douglas, Charles. *Natural History Notebook.* University of Chicago Press, 1980.
Hillcourt, William. *The New Field Book of Nature Activities and Hobbies.* Putnam, 1978.
Karstad, Aleta. *Wild Habitats.* Scribner, 1979.
Kilham, Lawrence. *A Naturalist's Field Guide.* Stackpole, 1981.
Muir, John. *Wilderness Essays.* Peregrine Smith, 1980.
Palmer, E. Lawrence, and H. Seymour Fowler. *Fieldbook of Natural History.* McGraw-Hill, 1975.

NATURAL HISTORY OF SPECIAL AREAS

Allen, Durward. *Life of Prairies and Plains.* McGraw-Hill, 1967.
The American Wildlife Region Series. 1954 to present. Books on wildlife and common plants of lowland California, the Sierras, the Northwest Pacific Coast, the Intermountain West, the Cas-

138

cades, the Northern Rocky Mountains, the Southern Rocky Mountains and the Intermountain West. Naturegraph.

Bedicheck, Roy. *Adventures with a Texas Naturalist.* University of Texas Press, 1961.

Brown, Vinson. *Field Guide of the Golden Sunbelt.* Prentice-Hall, (in press).

Cart, Archie. *The Everglades.* Time-Life, 1973.

Clark, Champ. *The Badlands.* Time-Life, 1975.

Clement, Roland. *Nature Atlas of America,* 2nd ed. Hammond, 1976.

Conrader, Jay, and Constance Conrader. *The Northwoods Wildlife Region.* Naturegraph, 1984.

Jorgensen, Neil. *Sierra Club's Naturalist Guide to Southern New England.* Sierra Club Books, 1978.

Kelley, Don. *Edge of a Continent: The Pacific Coast from Alaska to Baja.* American West, 1971.

Leonard, Jonathan. *Atlantic Beaches.* Time-Life, 1972.

Rabkin, Richard, and Jacob Rabkin. *Nature Guide to Florida.* Banyan, 1978.

Tanner, Ogden. *New England Wilds.* Time-Life, 1974.

BIOLOGY

Allred, Donald M. *Living Things: An Introduction to Natural History.* Brigham, 1974.

Applewhite, Philip. *Understanding Biology.* Holt, Rinehart & Winston.

Behnke, John A. *Challenging Biological Problems: Directions Towards Their Solutions.* Oxford University Press, 1972.

Behringer, Marjorie P. *Techniques & Materials In Biology.* Krieger, 1973.

Holland, et al. *Laboratory Explorations in General Biology.* Kendall/Hunt, 1977.

Kelly, James I., and Allan R. Orr. *Self-Pacing Biology Experiences.* Iowa State University Press, 1980.

INVERTEBRATES

Barth, Robert H. *The Invertebrate World.* Holt, Rinehart & Winston, 1981.

Brusca, Gary J. *General Patterns of Invertebrate Development.* Mad River, 1975.
Buchsbaum, Ralph. *Animals Without Backbones.* 2nd ed. University of Chicago Press, 1975.
Prasad, S.N. *Life of Invertebrates.* Advent, 1980.

ECOLOGY AND CONSERVATION

Barnett, Winston, and Cyril Winskell. *A Study in Conservation.* Routledge & Kegan Paul, 1978.
Berry, Brian J., and John D. Kasards. *Contemporary Urban Ecology.* Macmillan, 1977.
Buchsbaum, Ralph, and Mildred Buchsbaum. *Basic Ecology,* 4th ed. Boxwood Press, 1957.
Cairns, John, and Kenneth Dickson. *Recovery and Restoration of Damaged Ecosystems.* University Press of Virginia, 1977.
Caldwell, Lynton K., et al. *Citizens and the Environment: Case Studies in Popular Action.* Indiana University Press, 1976.
Collier, Boyd, et al. *Dynamic Ecology.* Prentice-Hall, 1973.
Davis, Ray J. *Ecology and Conservation of Natural Resources.* Clark, 1978.
Dubos, René. *The Resilience of Ecosystems.* Colorado Association, 1978.
Milne, Lorus J. and Margery Milne. *Ecology Out of Joint: New Environments and Why They Happen.* Scribner, 1977.
Owen, Oliver. *Natural Resource Conservation: An Ecological Approach,* 2nd ed. Macmillan, 1975.
Velaskasis, Kimon. *The Conserver Society: A Blueprint for the Future.* Harper & Row, 1979.

MAMMALS

Brown, Vinson. *Sea Mammals and Reptiles of the Pacific Coast,* rev. ed. Binford & Morts, 1984.
Burt, William H. *A Field Guide to the Mammals,* 3rd ed. Houghton Mifflin, 1976.
Hall, E. Raymond. *Mammals of North America,* 2 vols., 2nd ed. Wiley, 1981.
Nowak, Ronald, et al. *Wild Animals of North America.* National Geographic, 1979.

Whitaker, John O. *The Audubon Field Guide to North American Mammals.* Knopf, 1980.

BIRDS

Brown, Vinson, Henry Weston, Jr., and Jerry Buzzell. *Handbook of California Birds.* Naturegraph, 1979.

Curtis, Jane, and Will Curtis. *Welcome the Birds to Your Home.* Greene, 1980.

McElroy, Thomas P. *The Habitat Guide to Birding.* Knopf, 1974.

Massachusetts Audubon Society. *Birds of Western North America.* Greene, 1981.

Peterson, Roger T. *A Field Guide to the Birds East of the Rockies,* 4th ed. Houghton Mifflin, 1980.

Peterson, Roger T. *Field Guide to Western Birds.* Houghton Mifflin, 1972.

REPTILES AND AMPHIBIANS

Brown, Vinson. *Reptiles and Amphibians of the West.* Naturegraph, 1974.

Cochran, Doris M., and Coleman J. Goin. *The New Field Book of Reptiles and Amphibians.* Putnam, 1978.

Conant, Roger. *A Field Guide to Reptiles and Amphibians of Eastern and Central North America.* Houghton Mifflin, 1975.

King, F. Wayne, and John Baylor. *The Audubon Society Field Guide to North American Reptiles and Amphibians.* Knopf, 1979.

Stebbins, Robert C. *A Field Guide to Western Reptiles and Amphibians.* Houghton Mifflin, 1966.

POND AND STREAM LIFE

Andres, W. *Guide to the Study of Fresh Water Ecology.* Prentice-Hall, 1971.

Klotts, Elsie B. *The New Field Book of Fresh Water Life.* G.P. Putnam's, 1966.

Moss, Brian. *The Ecology of Fresh Waters.* Halsted Press, 1980.

Pennak, Robert W. *Fresh Water Invertebrates of the United States,* 2nd ed. Wiley, 1978.

Prescott, G.W. *How to Know the Fresh Water Algae,* 3rd ed. Wm. C. Brown, 1978.

Usinger, Robert L. *Life of Rivers and Streams.* McGraw-Hill, 1967.

Weller, Milton. *Freshwater Marshes: Ecology and Wildlife Management.* University of Minnesota Press, 1981.

MARINE LIFE

Abbot, Isabella, and E. Yale Dawson. *How to Know the Seaweeds,* 2nd ed. Wm. C. Brown, 1978.

Behrens, David. *Pacific Coast Nudibranches.* Western Marine, 1980.

Braun, Earnest, and Vinson Brown. *Exploring Pacific Coast Tide Pools.* Naturegraph, 1966.

Brown, Vinson. *Sea Mammals and Reptiles of the Pacific Coast.* Macmillan, 1976.

Burton, Robert. *The Seashore (Atlantic Coast).* G.P. Putnam's, 1977.

Carefoot, Thomas. *Pacific Seashores: A Guide to Intertidal Ecology.* University of Washington Press, 1977.

Guberlet, Muriel L. *Animals of the Seashore (Pacific Coast),* 4th ed. Binford & Morts, 1978.

———. *Seaweeds at Ebb Tide (Pacific Coast).* University of Washington Press, 1956.

Hedgpeth, Joel. *Common Seashore Life of Southern California.* Naturegraph, 1961.

Johnson, Myrtle, and Harry Snook. *Seashore Animals of the Pacific Coast.* Dover, 1967.

McLachlan, Dan, and Jack Ayres. *Fieldbook of Pacific Northwest Sea Creatures.* Naturegraph, 1979.

Moe, Martin A., Jr. *The Marine Aquarium Handbook.* Norns, 1981.

North, Wheeler. *Underwater California.* University of California Press, 1976.

Ricketts, Edward F., and Jack Calvin. *Between Pacific Tides,* 4th ed. Stanford University Press, 1968.

Smith, Lynwood. *Living Shores of the Pacific Northwest.* Pacific Search Press, 1976.

———. *Common Seashore Life of the Pacific Northwest.* Naturegraph, 1962.

Steele, John H. *The Structure of Marine Ecosystems.* Harvard University Press, 1977.

INSECTS

Borror, Donald L, and Richard H. White. *Field Guide to the Insects of America North of Mexico.* Houghton Mifflin, 1970.

Milne, Lorus, and Marjory Milne. *The Audubon Society Field Guide to North American Insects and Spiders.* Knopf, 1980.

Social Insects

Brian, M.V., ed. *Production Ecology of Ants and Termites.* Cambridge University Press, 1977.

Butler, Colin C. *World of the Honeybee.* Taplinger, 1975.

Evans, Howard E., and Mary Eberhard. *Wasps.* University of Michigan Press, 1970.

Helfer, Jacques. *How to Know the Grasshoppers, Cockroaches, and Their Allies.* Wm. C. Brown, 1963.

Howse, P.E. *Termites: A Study in Social Behavior.* Humanities, 1970.

Larson, Peggy P., and Melvin W. Larson. *All about Ants.* T.Y. Crowell, 1976.

Oster, George S., and Edward O. Wilson. *Caste and Ecology in the Social Insects.* Princeton University Press, 1978.

Sudd, John H. *Introduction to the Behavior of Ants.* St. Martin's, 1967.

Von Fritsch, Karl. *Bees: Their Vision, Chemical Senses and Language.* Cornell University Press, 1971.

Wheeler, William M. *Ants: Their Structure, Development and Behavior.* Columbia University Press, 1960.

―――. *Fungus-Growing Ants of North America.* Dover, 1974.

Beetles

Evans, M.E. *The Life of Beetles.* Hafner, 1975.

Headstrom, Richard. *The Beetles of America,* New ed. A.S. Barnes, 1977.

Jacques, Harry E. *How to Know the Beetles.* Wm. C. Brown, 1951.

Patenent, Dorothy H., and Paul Schroder. *Beetles and How They Live.* Holiday, 1978.

Butterflies and Moths

Ehrlich, Paul, and Anne Ehrlich. *How to Know the Butterflies.* Wm. C. Brown, 1961.

Emmel, Thomas C. *Butterflies: Their World, Their Life Cycle, Their Behavior.* Knopf, 1975.

Holland, W.J. *The Moth Book.* rev. ed. Dover, 1968.

Perenti, Umberto. *The World of Butterflies and Moths.* Putnam, 1978.

Stokoe, W.J. *The Observer's Book of Butterflies.* Scribner, 1979.

Spiders

Comstock, John H. *The Spider Book,* rev. ed. by W.J. Gertsch. Comstock, 1948.

Gertsch, Willis J. *American Spiders,* 2nd ed. Van Nostrand Reinhold, 1979.

Kaston, E.J. *How to Know the Spiders,* 3rd ed. Wm. C. Brown, 1978.

Levi, Herbert, and Lorna Levi. *Spiders and Their Kin.* Western, 1969.

Ochler, Charles M. *Jumping Spiders.* Ohio Biological Survey, 1980.

PARASITES

Kennedy, C.B., ed. *Ecological Aspects of Parasitology.* Elsevier, 1976.

Meyer, Marvin C., and O. Wilford Olsen. *Essentials of Parasitology,* 2nd ed. Wm. C. Brown, 1975.

Olsen, O. Wilford. *Animal Parasites: Their Life Cycles and Ecology,* 3rd ed. University Park Press, 1974.

MICROSCOPIC LIFE AND MICROSCOPY

Bradbury, S. *The Microscope: Past and Present.* Pergamon, 1969.

Brandt, W.H. *The Student's Guide to Optical Microscopes.* Wm. Kaufmann, 1975.

Cairns, John, Jr. *Aquatic Microbial Communities.* Garland, 1977.

Carona, Philip. *The Microscope and How to Use It.* Gulf Publishing, 1970.

Geisert, Paul. *Understanding the Microscope.* Educational Methods, 1967.

Gerbett, J.W., and A.J. Bartlett. *Experimental Biology with Microorganisms.* Butterworth, 1972.

Headstrom, Richard. *Adventures with a Hand Lens.* Dover, 1976.

Johnson, Gaylord, Maurice Beilfeld, and Joel Beller. *Hunting with the Microscope*. Arco, 1974.

ANIMAL HABITS AND BEHAVIOR (ETHOLOGY)

Alcock, John. *Animal Behavior: An Evolutionary Approach,* 2nd ed. Sinauer Associates, 1979.

BenDavid-Val, Leah, et al. *Discover Wildlife in Your Backyard.* National Wildlife, 1977.

Bosnel, R.G., and J.F. Fish. *Animal Sonar Systems.* Plenum, 1980.

Cloudsley-Thompson, J.L. *Tooth and Claw: Defensive Strategies in the Animal World.* Biblio Dist., 1980.

Dewsbury, Donald A. *Comparative Animal Behavior.* McGraw-Hill, 1977.

Etkin, William, ed. *Social Behavior and Organization Among Vertebrates.* University of Chicago Press, 1964.

Ford, Barbara. *Animals That Use Tools.* Messner, 1978.

Hahn, Emily. *Look Who's Talking! Discoveries in Animal Communication.* T.Y. Crowell, 1978.

Hammond, A.E. *How Animals Solve Their Problems.* Carlton, 1981.

Klopfer, Peter H. *Behavioral Aspects of Ecology.* Prentice-Hall, 1975.

Milne, Lorus, et al. *The Secret Life of Animals: Pioneering Discoveries in Animal Behavior.* Dutton, 1975.

Wallace, Robert. *Ecology and Evolution of Animal Behavior,* 2nd ed. Goodyear Publishing, 1979.

Winter, Ruth. *Scent Talk Among Animals.* Lippincott, 1977.

PLANTS

Abrams, Leroy. *Illustrated Flora of the Pacific States,* 4 vols. Stanford University Press, 1960.

Britton, Nathaniel, and Addison Brown. *Illustrated Flora of the Northern United States, Canada and the British Possessions.* Dover, 1970.

Cronquist, Arthur. *Evolution and Classification of Flowering Plants.* Houghton Mifflin, 1968.

Cronquist, Arthur, et al. *Intermountain Flora: Vascular Plants of the Inter-Mountain West* Hafner, 1972.

Jacques, Harry E. *How to Know the Plant Families,* 2nd ed. Wm. C. Brown, 1948.

MacFarlane, Ruth B. *Collecting and Preserving Plants for Science and Pleasure.* Arco, 1984.

Nelson. *Handbook of Rocky Mountain Plants,* 2nd rev. ed. King, 1977.

Rydberg, Per. *Flora of the Prairies and Plains of Central North America.* Dover, 1971.

Small, John Kunkel. *Manual of Southeastern Flora.* Hafner, 1972.

Flowers

Condon, Geneal. *The Complete Book of Flower Preservation.* Prentice-Hall, 1977.

Davis, P.H., and Cullen J. Davis. *The Identification of Flowering Plant Families.* Cambridge University Press, 1979.

Hultman, G. Eric. *Trees, Shrubs and Flowers of the Midwest.* Contemporary Books, 1978.

Klein, Richard, and Deana Klein. *Flowering Plants: A Nature and Science Book of Experiments.* Natural History Press, 1968.

Neiring, William. *The Audubon Society Field Guide to North American Wildflowers: Eastern Region.* Knopf, 1979.

Spellenberg, Richard. *The Audubon Society Field Guide to North American Wildflowers: Western Region.* Knopf, 1979.

Treshow, Michael. *Environment and Plant Response.* McGraw-Hill, 1970.

Ferns, Mosses and Grasses

Bland, John. *Forests of Lilliput: The Realm of Mosses and Lichens.* Prentice-Hall, 1971.

Cobb, Houghton. *A Field Guide to the Ferns and Their Related Families.* Houghton Mifflin, 1971.

Conrad, Henry. *How to Know the Mosses and Liverworts,* 2nd rev. ed. Wm. C. Brown, 1979.

Frye, Theodore. *Ferns of the Northwest.* Binford & Mort, 1977.

Grout, A.J. *Mosses with Hand Lens and Microscope.* J. Johnson, 1972.

Harrington, H.D. *How to Identify Grasses and Grass-like Plants.* Swallow Press, 1977.

Knobel, Edward. *Field Guide to the Grasses, Sedges and Rushes of the United States.* Dover, 1971.

Fungi

McKenny, Margaret. *The Savory Wild Mushroom,* rev. ed. University of Washington Press, 1971.

Miller, Orson K., Jr. *Mushrooms of North America,* rev. ed. Dutton, 1979.

Orr, Robert T. *Mushrooms of Western North America.* University of California Press, 1980.

Trees and Shrubs

Baerg, Harry. *How to Know the Western Trees,* 2nd ed. Wm. C. Brown, 1973.

Brown, Vinson. *Reading the Woods.* Macmillan, 1963.

Edlin, Herbert L. *The Tree Key.* Charles Scribner's, 1978.

Elias, Thomas. *The Complete Trees of North America Field Guide and Natural History.* Van Nostrand Reinhold, 1980. Excellent.

Krobel, Edward. *Identify Trees and Shrubs by Their Leaves.* Dover, 1972.

Millard, Howard. *How to Know the Trees (Eastern).* Wm. C. Brown, 1978.

Nader, Ira B., and Cornelia Oberlander. *Trees in the City.* Pergamon, 1978.

EARTH HISTORY AND FOSSILS

Beerbower, James R. *Field Guide to the Fossils.* Houghton Mifflin, 1971.

Casanova, Richard L., and Ronald P. Ratkovitch. *An Illustrated Guide to Fossil Collecting,* 3rd rev. ed. Naturegraph, 1982.

Hallam, A., ed. *Patterns of Evolution: As Illustrated by the Fossil Record.* Elsevier, 1977.

Lambert, Mark. *Fossils.* Arco, 1979.

Lane, N. Gary, *Life of the Past.* Merrill, 1978.

Leakey, Richard E. *The Making of Mankind.* Dutton, 1981.

Matthew, William D. *Climate and Evolution.* Arno, 1974.

Schopf, Thomas J. *Models in Paleobiology.* W.H. Freeman, 1972.

ROCKS, MINERALS AND LAND FORMS

Atkinson, Richard, and Frances Atkinson. *The Observer's Book of Rocks and Minerals.* Scribner, 1979.

Brown, Vinson, and David Allen II. *An Illustrated Guide to Common Rocks and Rock-Forming Minerals.* Naturegraph, 1976.

————. *Rocks and Minerals of California,* 3rd ed. Naturegraph, 1972.

ASTRONOMY

Apfel, Necia. *Astronomy Projects for Young Scientists.* Arco, 1984.

Beattles, J. Kelley, et al. *The New Solar System.* Cambridge University Press, 1981.

Beet, E.A. *Mathematical Astronomy for Amateurs.* Norton, 1972.

Capt, E. Raymond. *The Glory of the Stars.* Artisan Sales, 1976.

Christianson, Gale E. *The Wild Abyss: The Story of the Men Who Made Modern Astronomy.* Free Press, 1979.

Claiborne, Robert. *The Summer Stargazer: Astronomy for Beginners.* Penguin, 1981.

Fanning, Anthony E. *Planets, Stars and Galaxies: Descriptive Astronomy for Beginners.* Peter Smith, 1966.

Gingerich, Owen. *New Frontiers in Astronomy: Readings from Scientific American.* W.H. Freeman, 1975.

Greenleaf, Peter. *Experiments in Space Science.* Arco, 1980.

Gribbin, John. *Amateur Astronomer.* Smith, 1979.

Henbest, Nigel. *The Exploding Universe.* Macmillan, 1979.

Hopkins, Joanne, ed. *Glossary of Astronomy and Astrophysics.* University of Chicago Press, 1976. Good for finding meanings of terms.

Jones, Aubrey. *Mathematical Astronomy with a Pocket Calculator.* Halsted, 1979.

Knox, Richard. *Experiments in Astronomy for Amateurs.* St. Martin's, 1979.

Muirden, James. *Astronomy with Binoculars.* Arco, 1983.

Mundt, Carlos. *Stars and Outer Space Made Easy.* Naturegraph, 1966.

Rickert, Russell K. *Astronomy and Space Exploration.* Addison-Wesley, 1974.

Ridpath, Ian. *The Young Astronomer's Handbook.* Arco, 1984.
Sidgwick, J.B. *Amateur Astronomer's Handbook.* Dover, 1981.
Vehrenberg, Hans. *Atlas of Deep Sky Splendors,* 4th ed. Sky, 1978.
Verschuur, Gerrit L. *Cosmic Catastrophies.* Addison-Wesley, 1978.
Wervill, Roy. *Stars and Telescopes for the Beginner.* Taplinger, 1980.

ARCHAEOLOGY

Barker, Philip. *The Techniques of Archaeological Excavation.* Universe, 1977.
Bradford, John. *Ancient Landscape Studies in Field Archeology.* Greenwood, 1950.
Caso, Antonio. *Thirteen Masterpieces of Mexican Archaeology.* Gordon, 1976.
Ceram, C.W. *The First American: A Story of North American Archeology.* NAL, 1972.
Martin, Paul S., et al. *Indians Before Columbus: Twenty Thousand Years of North American History Revealed by Archaeology.* University of Chicago Press, 1947.
A New Look at Mysteries of Archaeology. Arco, 1980.
A New Look at Treasures of Archaeology. Arco, 1980.
Woodall, Ned J. *An Introduction to Modern Archaeology.* Schenkman, 1972.

AMERICAN INDIANS

Alexander, Hartley B. *World's Rim: Great Mysteries of the North American Indians.* University of Nebraska Press, 1967.
Brown, Vinson. *Native Americans of the Pacific Coast.* Naturegraph, 1984.
Densmore, Frances. *How Indians Use Wild Plants for Food, Medicine and Crafts.* Dover, 1974.
Driver, Harold E. *Indians of North America,* 2nd rev. ed. University of Chicago Press, 1969.
————, and William C. Massey. *Comparative Studies of North American Indians.* American Philosophy, 1975.
Grey Owl and Little Pigeon. *Cry of the Ancients.* Herald House, 1974.

Heizer, Robert F. and M.A. Whipple, eds. *The California Indians: A Source Book.* University of California Press, 1971.

Kroeber, Theodora. *Ishi in Two Worlds: A Biography of the Last Wild Indian in North America.* University of California Press, 1961.

Mails, Thomas E. *Mystic Warriors of the Plains.* Doubleday, 1972.

Spencer, Robert F., et al. *The Native Americans: Ethnology and Backgrounds of the North American Indians.* Harper & Row, 1977.

Waldman, Harry, ed. *Encyclopedia of Indians of the Americas.* Scholarly Press, 1974–81.

Wissler, Clark. *Relation of Nature to Man in Aboriginal America.* AMS Press, 1926.

The World of the American Indian. National Geographic, 1974.

MOUNTING AND DISSECTING SPECIMENS

Berman, William. *How to Dissect,* 4th ed. Arco, 1984.

Grantz, Gerald J. *Home Book of Taxidermy and Tanning.* Stackpole, 1970.

Harden, Cleo. *How to Preserve Animals and Other Specimens in Clear Plastic.* Naturegraph, 1963.

Haynes, Michael D. *Haynes on Air Brush Taxidermy.* Arco, 1979.

McFall, Waddy F. *Taxidermy Step By Step.* Winchester Press, 1975.

Peterson, Alva. *Entomological Techniques,* 10th ed. Entomological Rep., 1964.

Roberts, Nadine H. *The Complete Handbook of Taxidermy.* TAB Books, 1979.

NATURE PHOTOGRAPHY

Angel, Heather. *Nature Photography: Its Art and Techniques.* International Publications Service, 1972.

Bauer, Erwin A. *Outdoor Photography,* 2nd ed. Dutton, 1980.

Freeman, Michael. *The Complete Book of Wildlife and Nature Photography.* Simon & Schuster, 1981.

Kinne, Russ. *The Complete Book of Nature Photography,* 3rd ed. Amphoto, 1979.

Maye, Patricia. *Fieldbook of Nature Photography.* Sierra Club Books, 1974.
Pfiffer, C. Boyd. *Field Guide to Outdoor Photography.* Stackpole, 1977.
Wooters, John, and Jerry Smith. *Wildlife Images: A Complete Guide to Outdoor Photography.* Petersen, 1981.

CARVING AND SCULPTING

Beecroft, Glennis. *Carving Techniques.* Watson-Guptill, 1976.
Green, H.D. *Carving Realistic Birds.* Peter Smith, 1978.
Hanna, Jay. *Marine Carving Handbook.* International Marine, 1975.
Prince, Arnold. *Carving Wood and Stone.* Prentice-Hall, 1981.
Tawes, William I. *Creative Sculpture.* Cornell Maritime, 1976.

DRAWING AND PAINTING

Calderon, W. Frank. *Animal Painting and Anatomy.* Dover, 1975.
Coleridge, Sarah. *Painting Flowers in Water Color.* Taplinger, 1981.
Dember, Sol, et al. *Drawing and Painting the World of Animals.* H.W. Sams, 1977.
Jameson, Kenneth. *Flower Painting for Beginners.* Taplinger, 1979.
Leslie, Clare W. *Nature Drawing: A Tool for Learning.* Prentice-Hall, 1980.
Shofield, Heather. *Flower Painting Techniques.* Larousse, 1979.
Wilwerding, W.J. *Animal Drawing and Painting,* rev. ed. Peter Smith, 1966.

LETTERING

Ballinger, Raymond. *Lettering Art in Modern Use.* Van Nostrand Reinhold, 1979.
Benson, John H. and A.G. Carey. *Elements of Lettering,* 2nd ed. McGraw-Hill, 1962.
Biegeleison, J.I. *The ABC of Lettering,* 5th ed. Harper & Row, 1976.
Mitchell, Frederick. *Practical Lettering and Layout,* 2nd ed. Dufour, 1960.
Semere, Mario G. *A Guide to Hand Lettering.* Kendall/Hunt, 1977.

WOODWORKING

Blanford, Percy. *The Woodworker's Bible.* TAB Books, 1981.
————. *The Master Handbook of Fine Woodworking Techniques & Projects.* Tab Books, 1981.
Broadwater, Elaine. *Woodburning: Art and Craft.* Crown, 1980.
Jones, Bernard E. *The Complete Woodworker.* Ten Speed Press, 1980.
Maguire, Byron. *The Complete Book of Woodworking and Cabinet-Making.* Reston, 1974.

MODELS AND MODELING

Angle, B., ed. *Hints and Tips for Plastic Modelers.* Plenum, 1975.
Berensohn, Paulus. *Finding One's Way with Clay.* Simon & Schuster, 1972.
Guide to Clay Modelling. British Culture Center, 1976.
Helfman, Harry. *Making Your Own Sculpture.* Morrow, 1971.
Kallenberg, Lawrence. *Model in Wax for Jewelry & Sculpture.* Chilton, 1981.
Kenny, John B. *Ceramic Sculpture.* Chilton, 1953.
Kowall, Dennis, Jr., and Donna Meilach. *Sculpture Casting.* Crown, 1972.
Miller, Richard M. *Figure Sculpture in Wax and Plaster.* Watson-Guptill, 1971.
Newman, Thelma R. *Crafting with Plastics.* Chilton, 1975.
Scarfe, Herbert. *Crafts in Polyester Resin.* Watson-Guptill, 1973.
Zaidenberg, Arthur. *The Lively Way to Modeling Sculpture: A Book for Beginners.* Vanguard, 1982.
Zechlin, Katherina. *Setting in Clear Plastic.* Taplinger, 1972.
Zeier, Franz. *Paper Constructions: Two- and Three-Dimensional Forms for Artists, Architects and Designers.* Scribner, 1980.

Appendix C

Where to Get Supplies

SCIENTIFIC SUPPLY HOUSES

Scientific supply houses can supply you with many specimens and tools for exhibits, as well as books, kits, chemicals, and equipment such as microscopes. These companies' catalogues may also give you ideas for exhibits and projects. A partial list of companies follows.

Berkshire Biological Supply Company, P.O. Box 404, Florence, MA 01060-0404

California Biological Service, 1212 W. Glendale Blvd., Glendale, CA 91201

Carolina Biological Supply Company, 2700 York Rd., Burlington, NC 27215

Central Scientific Company, 2600 S. Kostner Ave., Chicago, IL 60623

College Biological Supply Company, 8857 Mt. Israel Rd., Escondido, CA 92025

Connecticut Valley Biological Supply Company, P.O. Box 326, Southampton, MA 01073

Earth Science Materials, Inc., P.O. Box 69, Florence, CO 81226

Fisher Scientific Company, Educational Division, 4901 W. Le Moyne St., Chicago, IL 60651

Frey Scientific Company, 905 Hickory La., Mansfield, OH 44905

Lab-Aids, Inc., 130 Wilbur Pl., Bohemia, NY 11716

LaPine Scientific Company, 6001 S. Knox Ave., Chicago, IL 60629-5496

Macmillan Scientific Company, 8200 S. Hoyne Ave., Chicago, IL 60620

McKilligan Supply Corporation, 435 Main St., Johnson City, NY 13790

NASCO, 901 Janesville Ave., Fort Atkinson, WI 53538

153

Sargent-Welch Scientific Company, 7300 N. Linder Ave., Skokie, IL 60077

School-Tech Inc., 745 State Circle, Box 1941, Ann Arbor, MI 48104

Science Kit, Inc., 777 E. Park Dr., Tonawanda, NY 14150

Southern Biological Supply Company, P.O. Box 68, McKenzie, TN 38201

Standard Scientific Supply Corporation, 30 Turner Pl., Piscataway, NJ 08854

Ward's Natural Science Establishment, Box 1712, Rochester, NY 14603

A large list of suppliers, the *Directory of Science Education Suppliers,* can be obtained by sending five dollars to the National Science Teachers Association, 1742 Connecticut Ave., N.W., Washington, DC 20009.

SUPPLIERS OF MATERIALS, SPECIMENS AND SERVICES

Following is a list of companies or organizations that provide special products, specimens and services—usually a more limited variety of products than the supply houses. Write for a complete catalogue. The list is organized by product or service.

Bowls, Mixing; Burs, Grinding; Misc. Equipment

Dick Ells Co.
908 Venice Blvd.
Los Angeles, CA 90015
(213) 747-5129

Brushes, Artists' Paint

Utrecht Linen, Inc.
36 A. Third Ave.
New York, NY 10003
(212) 777-5353

Clay, Modeling
("Roma Italian Plastilina")

Standard Clay Mines
38 E. 30th St.
New York, NY 10016
(212) 679-7474

Excelsior

J.W. Elwood Supply Co.
1202 Howard St.
Omaha, NB 68102
(402) 342-2221

Eyes, Glass Animal

Jonas Bros., Inc.
1037 Broadway
Denver, CO 80203
(303) 255-4813

Molding Compounds

Jeltrate-Type 1, Dental Impression Molding Material
Shaw Dental Supply
Div. D.L. Saslow Co.
1040 South Flower
Los Angeles, CA 90015
(213) 748-9234

Latex Rubber
A-R Products
11935 E. Washington Blvd.
Whittier, CA 90606
(213) 695-3008

Plaster, Hydrostone, Ultrocal-30
Westwood Ceramic Supply Co.
14400 Lomitas Ave.
City of Industry, CA 91744
(213) 330-0631

Silicone RTV Rubber
Dow Corning RTV Silicone
E.V. Roberts Co.
8500 Steller Dr.
Culver City, CA 90230
(213) 870-9561

Hastings RTV Silicone
Hastings Plastics Co.
1704 Colorado Ave.
Santa Monica, CA 90404
(213) 829-3449

Newsletter, Freeze Drying

Dr. Roland Hower
Freeze Dry Lab
National Museum of Natural History
Washington, D.C. 20418
(202) 357-1300

Paints

Acrylic, Oil, Watercolor
Utrecht Linens, Inc.
36 A. Third Ave.
New York, NY 10003
(212) 777-5353

Lacquer
Thompson Lacquer Co., Inc.
2324 S. Grand Ave.
Los Angeles, CA 90007
(213) 746-1421

Paint Sprayer

Binks Mfg. Co.
2553 S. Garfield Ave.
Los Angeles, CA 90040
(213) 685-4560

Polyester Resin, Mat Fiber, Chip Fiber

Berton Plastics
170 Wesley St., Box 1906
South Hackensack, NJ 07606

Cementex Latex Corporation
480 Canal St.
New York, NY 10013
(212) 226-5832

Polyester Resins, "Air Curve Flexible Slip" and Other Molding Compounds

Douglas and Sturgess
475 Bryant St.
San Francisco, CA 94107

Small Hand Tools

Friedheim Tool Supply Co.
412 W. 6th St.
Los Angeles, CA 90014
(213) 628-4174

Sportys Tool Shop
Clermont Country Airport
Batavia, OH 45103
(513) 732-2411

Specimens, Animal

Local Zoological Parks
U.S. Fish and Wildlife Service
Local Fish and Game Dept.
U.S. Customs Service
Local Animal Shelters

Index

Italic numbers refer to illustrations.

ARCO BOOKS FOR THE YOUNG SCIENTIST